NORTH

Nicolas Vanier

NORTH

Adventures in the Frozen Wild

Translated from the French by Willard Wood

Harry N. Abrams, Inc., Publishers

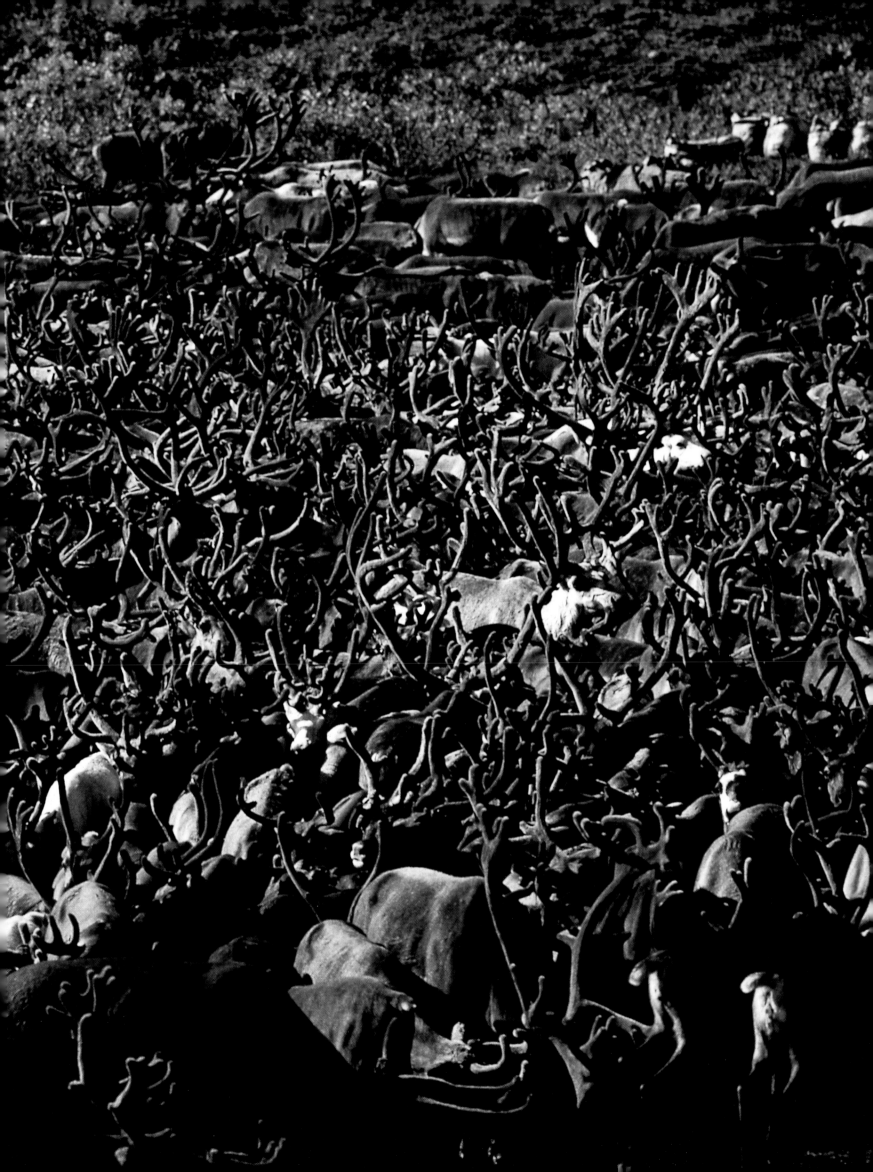

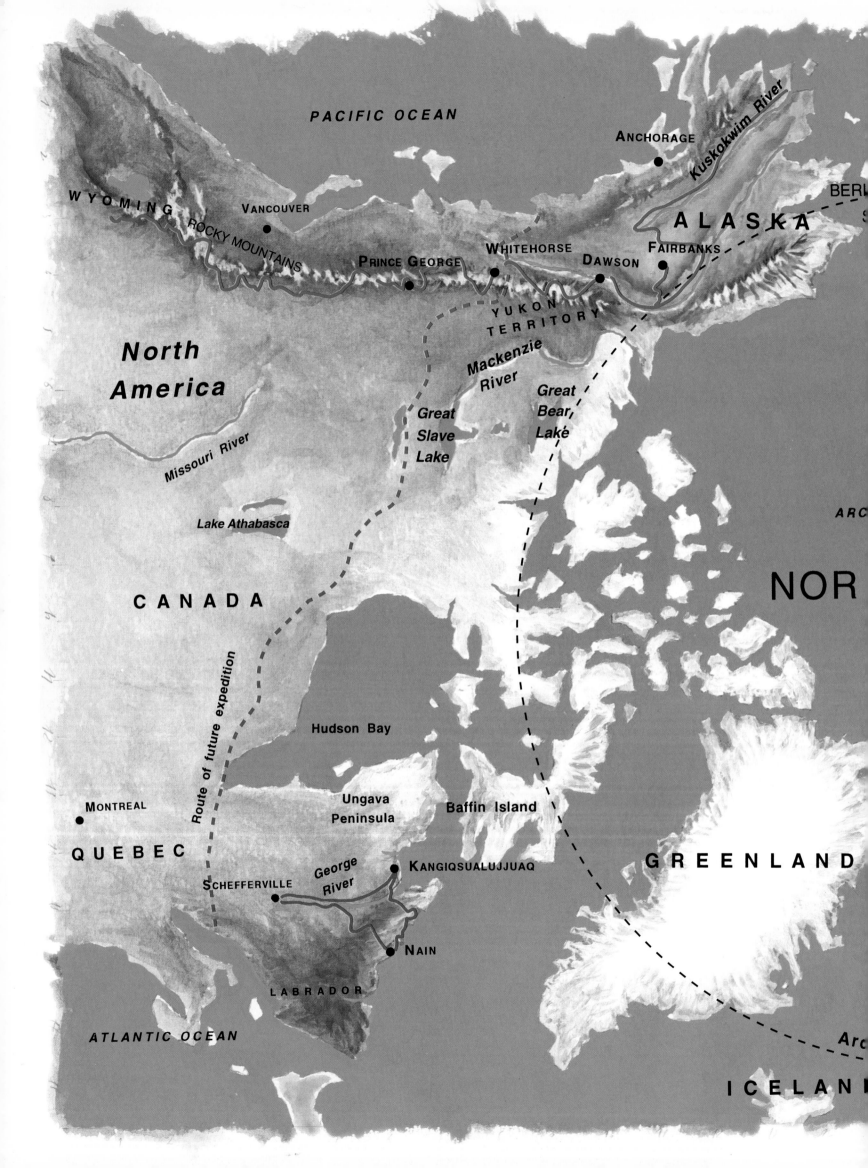

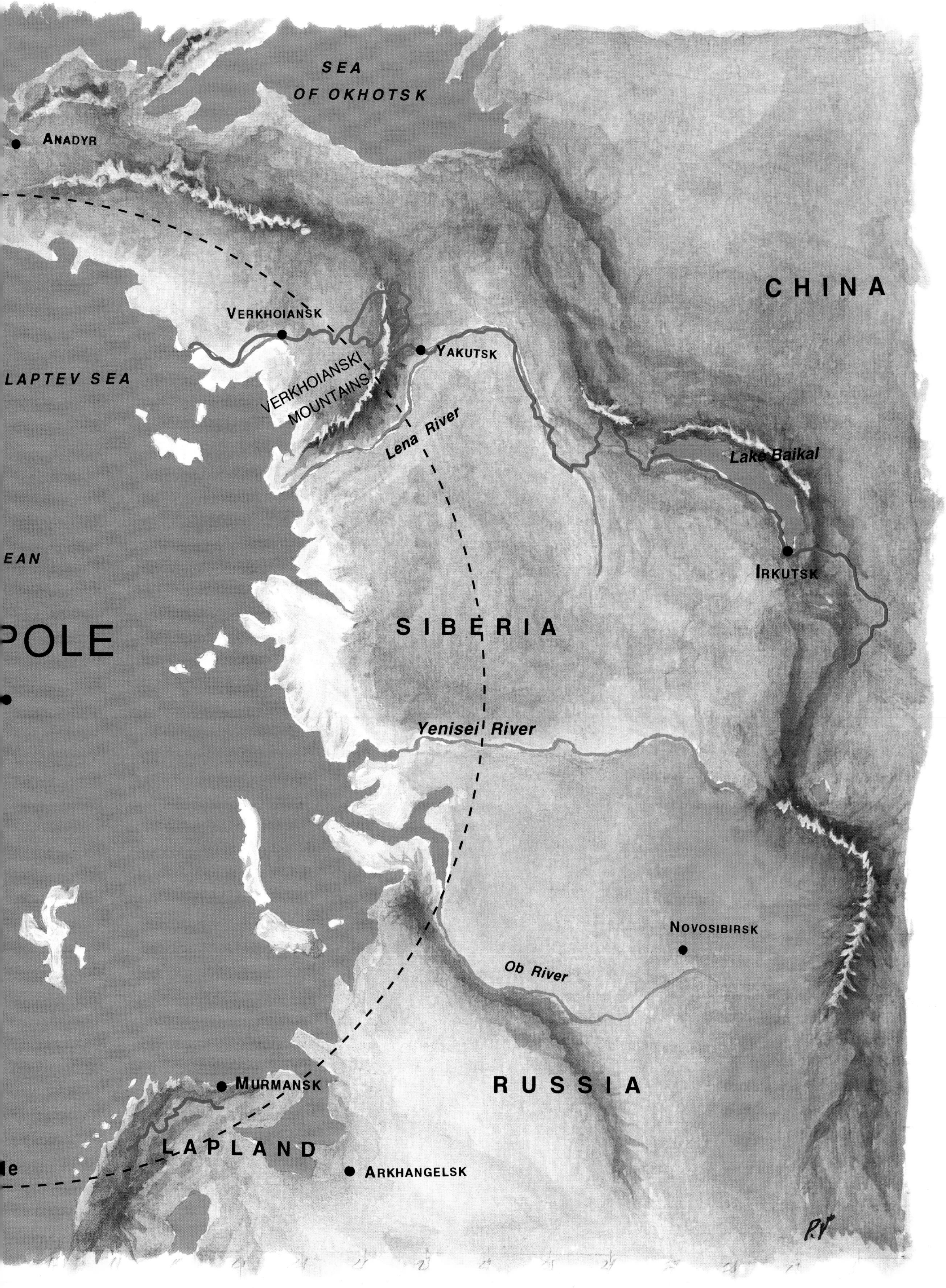

SEA
OF OKHOTSK

ANADYR

CHINA

VERKHOIANSK

LAPTEV SEA

YAKUTSK

VERKHOIANSKI
MOUNTAINS

Lake Baikal

Lena River

EAN

IRKUTSK

POLE

SIBERIA

Yenisei River

NOVOSIBIRSK

Ob River

RUSSIA

MURMANSK

LAPLAND

ARKHANGELSK

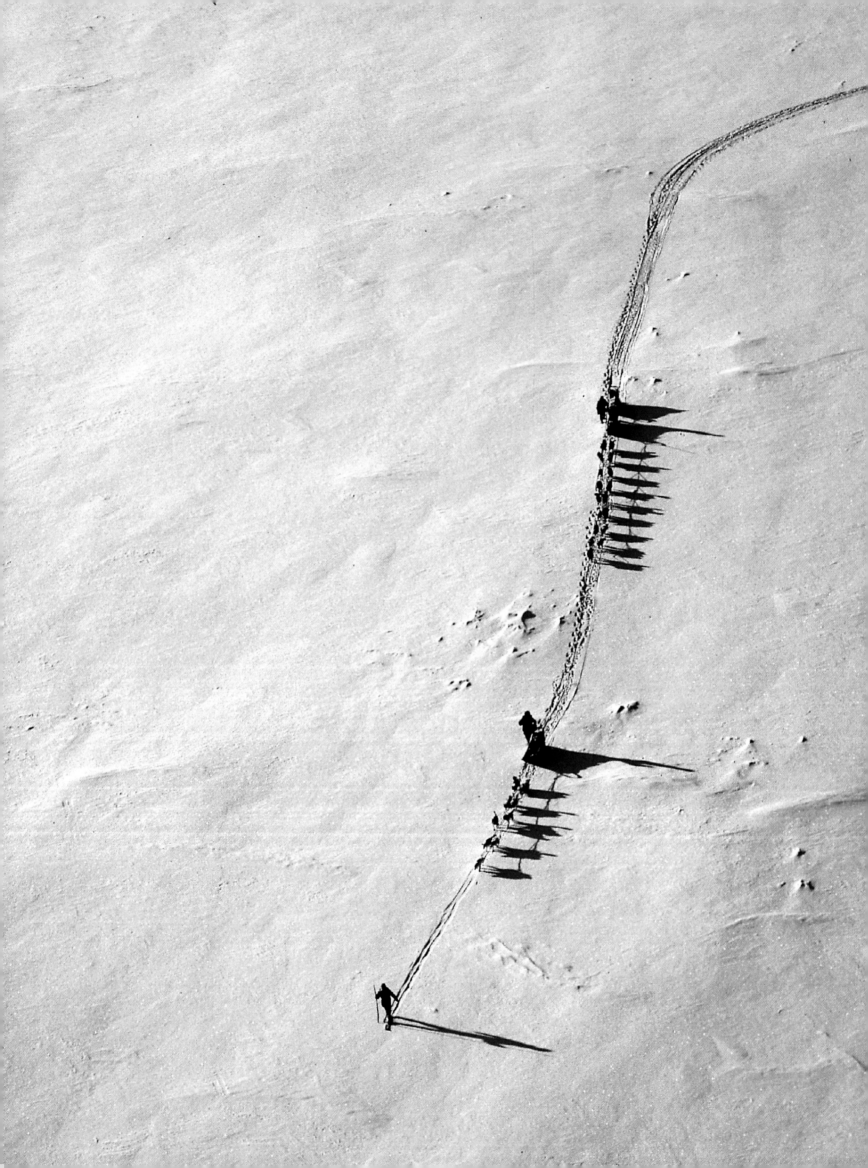

CONTENTS

PREFACE

THE PHOTOGRAPHS at the beginning and end of this book were taken twenty years apart.

After having dreamt of the Far North as a child, I have been able to visit it at every stage of my life as a man—at sixteen, at eighteen, at twenty, and then at thirty and beyond. I have gone there many times, and will continue to do so until my strength fails me.

In all these years, I've changed traveling companions often: Benoît, Alain, Totoche, Volodya, Nicolaï—the names that stud the pages of this book and the faces they belong to, fleeting but unforgettable, are those of childhood friends, of expedition partners, or of natives who became friends. With them I was able to form ever-different and ever-nourishing ties, because the Far North strips men down and makes it impossible for them to have purely conventional relationships. This is true even when the team members can't stand each other anymore, and every word spoken and every inch covered is poisoned by hostility, which has also happened.

Then there are my father, my wife, and Montaine, my daughter. The generations have come full circle. Although I was not born in the north countries, I have always wanted to bring those closest to me there, to make them see what has driven me and haunted me so long, so that they might understand, share my enthusiasms, and forgive some of my foibles.

The Far North is also that gallery of presences—some distant, some familiar—lining the course of the last twenty years—presences that accompany me in the great white solitudes and watch over me. These twenty years have no existence for me, given that all these trips were atemporal and join to form a single journey in my soul.

If you travel by canoe or dogsled and live in the forest, today's experience can be similar to that of the eighteenth century—but only on the condition that you use exclusively natural materials (wood, leather, fur). To be outside time and history, with the illusion of being suspended far above the many epochs and ages, is one of the great privileges nature affords those who put themselves in her power.

The ravages of civilization have taken their toll in villages and even more obviously in cities, but I made the choice to avoid showing anything in this book that jars with the landscape. In consequence, I have used only a few lovely images of Indian, Inuit, and Siberian villages. The desire for harmony needs always to be strengthened if the process of forgetting, which overwhelms us in our urban lives, is to be checked.

I am neither an adventurer, a scientist, nor an explorer. I am simply a man in love with nature at its wildest and most beautiful. I love all that lives there—plants, animals, and humans. I have no other motive for these distant expeditions unless it is the aim and inclination to show the world just how beautiful that nature is, particularly where it is best preserved because it is most inaccessible. My efforts may amount to no more than a drop in the ocean, yet I cling to the belief that the ocean needs that drop of water.

I could have lingered over the pulp mills that disfigure the southern shores of Lake Baikal and pollute the most transparent waters in the world, but I preferred to look at the lake's other shores. I could have told how, after I arrived by dogsled at an Inuit village, the schoolmaster asked me to take his students for a turn on the sea ice so that they wouldn't forget this traditional means of travel. I could have shown drunken or drugged Indians making their way from bar to bar, or Inuit villages made monstrous by concrete, but I have refrained and reveal nothing of all that.

My journeys prove nothing. They never attempt to break a record or make a first. In fact, they could more accurately be called "lasts," since no one travels by canoe or dogsled nowadays. Motorboats and snowmobiles are everywhere, not to mention 4 x 4s, which have invaded the Rocky Mountains and the mustang prairies of North America.

The territories that are inaccessible to motorized vehicles are destined to become uninhabited deserts. The rare few who might still be capable of living there no longer have the means to do so—the price of furs and gold have dropped too low. Yet a country without people is a country without soul. Those who resist, who refuse to abandon their ties to the environment and make it a point of honor to stay in harmony with nature, are in consequence all the more admirable. The people I have met in the north—the inhabitants of the Siberian arctic, for instance—have something to tell us, something as elementary as reading a track, listening to the wind, or watching an eagle describe circles in the sky. Perhaps elementary, but also fundamental. These small things speak to strong ties, and they are not just the fancies of diehard ecologists. They are something far different from a school of thought or an ideology. If we sever the umbilical cord that connects us to "Our Mother Earth," as the Indians call it, don't we run the risk of being cut off from ourselves and insidiously transforming our own world into a terrifying terra incognita?

Crossing the Quebec-Labrador Peninsula by Canoe

CANADA! For me, "Canada" was always a magic word, evocative of mystery and savage grandeur. Canada was everything. It was enormous spaces where you could walk for months, the books said, without seeing another living soul. It was also Jack London, wolves, great herds of caribou, dogsleds, the Northern Lights. It was all the things I had soaked up as a child looking through books and at pictures.

These dreams were finally going to take form for me and several of my childhood friends, with whom I had shared them.

Yet the story really starts with 100-pound sacks of coffee, and what could be more real than that? These were sacks—several thousand of them—that had to be moved between four AM and noon from the docks of Le Havre onto the trucks waiting to bring them to the warehouses. The job of part-time dockworker was fairly well paid. And the sacks of coffee, arriving from distant countries, exhaled a delicious smell of the far-off, encouraging us to earn our travel money. By the end of July we had enough to buy ourselves round-trip tickets to Montreal, bus tickets from Montreal to Sept-Iles, two canoes specially commissioned from the Montagnais Indians, train fare from Sept-Iles 350 miles north to Schefferville,

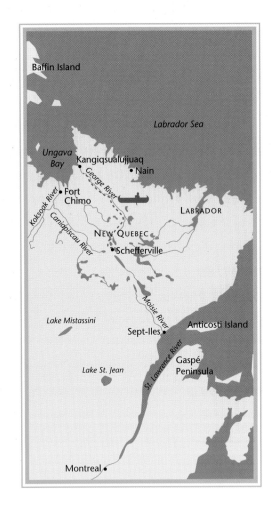

equipment, food, a canvas tent, fishing rods, and a gun—passports to a dream.

None of us slept a wink in the plane. Of the long journey from Montreal to Sept-Iles, at the mouth of the St. Lawrence River, all I can say is that we spent the entire time with our eyes glued to the windows of the train. Then came our meeting with the Indians, the delivery of our canoes, the train ride into the Far North and finally to the last settlement on the edge of no-man's-land. We traveled the last few miles with an Indian in a pickup truck, and he dropped us—and all our stuff—off on the edge of a great lake.

"Sure, you cross about twenty lakes, heading northeast. Between the lakes you portage all your gear. That should bring you to the Pas River, and you can follow that down to the sea. Be real careful in the rapids. We lost two more Indians in the river last year." A $100 bill changed hands, and the truck drove off.

Silence. Huge. The water lapping at the shore, the wind sifting through the pines, a few geese a long way off in the sky—nothing else. The emotion we felt was overpowering. Choking.

That was it. My life was linked to the Far North the way a man's destiny may be joined to a woman's from the moment their eyes meet.

Over short distances, a canoe can be carried in
this way, without a strap.

A childhood friend, Benoît Maury-Laribière has
been my partner on many adventures. We've
undergone a baptism of fire together—trekking
through Lapland, canoeing through Labrador,
riding through the Rockies, Siberia. . . . The list
is a long one. Today he runs the Laïka travel
agency in Paris, which specializes in hunting,
fishing, and adventure trips.

Near the ocean, an extraordinary stillness. The current is practically nil, and you have to paddle from morning to night to make any progress.

Traders and Missionaries

Changes brought to Labrador by fur traders and missionaries

The first Europeans to reach the coast of Labrador were undoubtedly Scandinavian Vikings, who landed more than a thousand years ago. Jacques Cartier sailed along the coast in 1534, reporting it to be "desolate and distressing." Captain Cook and other navigators shared that opinion, finding the country to be "of incredible poverty." The Indians and Inuit resided there quietly and would probably have continued to do so for several more centuries if missionaries and fur traders (whose purposes diverged but whose effects were disastrously similar) had not entered their remote territory.

The Indians, who used furs only to a limited extent, were too happy to exchange them for the white man's objects, not realizing where the trade would lead them. They gradually became so mired in debt that they were forced to trap more and more, neglecting the caribou that were their mainstay to chase after fur-bearing animals and, of course, European goods. In this way they became totally dependent on the trading companies, which set the prices on all commodities. As the region became depleted from overtrapping, terrible famines ensued.

While the fur trade was developing, missionaries were also establishing themselves in the area, using various means, many of them despicable, for winning over souls to their cause. Within a few decades the Indians had become sedentary and were dependent on whites for their alcohol, their food, and their religion. They had lost their strength and tribal identity. Even today they are still desperately looking for a door through which they may enter a world that is not their own.

Portaging, Building, and Lining a Canoe

The basic design of the canoe has not changed among the Montagnais, who still construct canoes to order, although canvas has taken the place of bark.

The birchbark canoe was lighter (65 as opposed to 110 pounds) and was therefore easier to portage, though it was less stable in the water. It was easy to fix if it ever got damaged, since all the elements of the "repair kit" could be found in the woods: bark, fiber from the root of the spruce tree, and pine gum. It was a trapper's canoe par excellence.

Canoe with a traditional ash frame and canvas skin.

Going Against the Current

In the wilderness, you don't always paddle with the current—in fact, you do so only half the time! To travel upriver you either paddle, pole, or use a technique called lining.

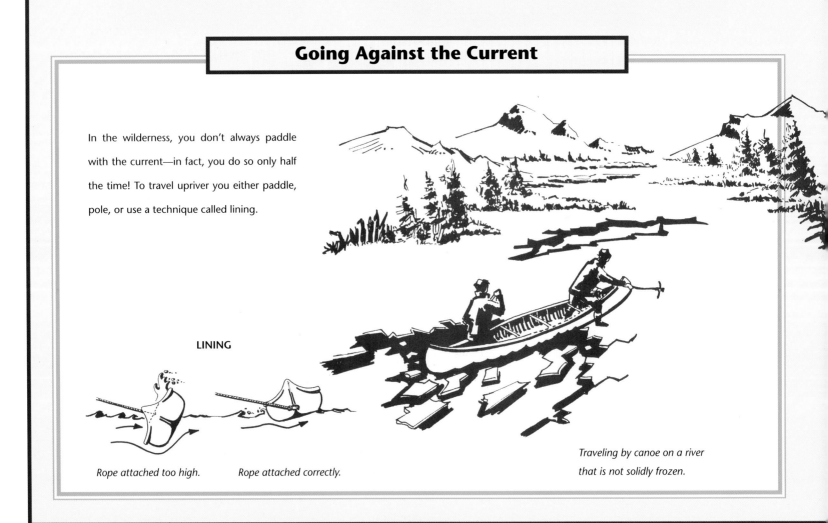

LINING

Rope attached too high.   *Rope attached correctly.*

Traveling by canoe on a river that is not solidly frozen.

PORTAGING

You put the strap on your head and the oars on your shoulders.

Before portaging a canoe any great distance, particularly when crossing a mountain range from one watershed to another, the craft must be dried to make it lighter.

Holding the gunwales guides the canoe and keeps it at the proper angle.

It's necessary to use a forehead strap or tumpline when carrying a load of more than ninety pounds.

What a trapper carried with him on a canoe journey at the beginning of the century. The equipment list remains unchanged today.

- a tent and a stove
- a gun, shells, and a few bullets
- a fishing rod, spoons, and spinners
- a small fishing net
- brass wire for rabbit snares
- canvas and glue for repairing the canoe
- twenty bottles of insect repellent
- an ax and a saw
- two cookpots, a grill, a frying pan
- ten boxes of mosquito coils
- a first-aid kit
- 220 pounds of flour and 1 pound of baking soda
- 44 pounds of lard
- 44 pounds of sugar
- 12 pounds of tea and coffee
- 7 pounds of salt
- 65 pounds of beans, rice, and noodles

God created Labrador in
six days, and on the seventh
he threw stones at it.

Labrador saying

*Lake Hutte Sauvage, halfway between
Schefferville and the Labrador coast. A strong
north wind often makes canoeing difficult.*

When traveling upriver, the Montagnais use a
long pole to propel the canoe and to keep its nose
pointed into the current. When they reach their
destination, they plant the pole into the lakebed,
just as others have already planted theirs.
These lakes are called "pole cemeteries."

The Montagnais Indians

Although they live in a region with an extensive network of lakes and
rivers and therefore travel largely by water, the Montagnais do not
know how to swim.

They belong to the People of the Snowshoe, a group that also includes the Déné
and the Algonquin. Despite differences in topography, climate, and environment—
which ranges from tundra to subarctic forest, from the Yukon to the Quebec-Labrador
peninsula—this part of the north has produced one type of human culture.

Caribou was long the main source of food and clothing for most of these peoples.
They followed the caribou migration, camping near their winter grounds to hunt and
supply themselves with food. The Montagnais therefore made a long canoe journey
every autumn, paddling or poling upriver with their prey. When the rivers were too low
or too swift, or had petered out entirely (for instance, between lakes), the Montagnais
portaged their canoes and equipment, carrying it all on their backs with the help of a
tumpline. Some Montagnais, who today rank among the strongest Indian porters, are
able to carry loads of more than four hundred pounds for distances of several miles.

James Bay Project

On November 11, 1975, the governments of Quebec and Canada, in conjunction with a number of the companies interested in building a dam project in the James Bay area (the southern extension of Hudson Bay), signed an agreement with the Indians and Inuit of arctic Quebec that allowed work on a giant hydroelectric plant to begin.

In exchange for ceding certain territories previously granted to them, the native peoples were to receive substantial payments, as well as exclusive hunting and fishing rights to comparable land elsewhere. The Indians and Inuit now receive monthly checks, making them financially dependent in a way that has aggravated the problems of alcohol, drugs, and depression. In many cases, these people no longer need to hunt or even work to survive; they have lost their pride—and their dignity.

Indians portaging their canoe and equipment to avoid dangerous rapids. Nineteenth-century engraving.

Bear cubs weigh barely a pound when they are born and are completely hairless! They grow quickly, however, and by the spring already weigh more than twenty pounds and are able to climb trees.

Fish is the staple food in the Far North, especially during the summer, when the water is free of ice. Meals take on a gigantic, almost obsessive, importance on an expedition. By early morning you are already thinking about what is for dinner, discussing it, and earnestly awaiting it. It is the one true meal of the day. Each person plays a part in preparing the menu according to a careful division of labor. Why the ritual? To eat, of course, but mealtime is also the opportunity to have a conversation, relax, and stop our incessant activity.

Meat makes up only a third of the expedition diet, unless we have been able to shoot big game—caribou, moose, or black bear.

During the summer, caribou spend a great deal of time in the water. Even if there is a very large lake in their path, they simply plunge right in and swim across it rather than walk around it—for one thing it provides them some relief from the mosquitoes. Caribou are excellent swimmers.

The willow ptarmigan is extraordinarily well camouflaged on the summer tundra. On the left, the female; on the right, the male.

By Dogsled Across Taiga, Tundra, and Sea Ice

WHEN YOUR GREAT LOVE is the Far North and you have never spent the winter there, you are a bit like an eagle enthusiast who has never seen an eagle in flight—you've missed the main part.

The Far North shows its true colors only when the cold has frozen the landscape solid and makes plumes of frost billow from people's mouths. Then it's the season for long dogsled journeys through the white wastelands, fur trapping, blizzards, and sea ice, and the time when wolf packs howl at the Northern Lights.

This is the Far North.

Having experienced summer there and learned to use the Indians' traditional means of transportation, I was now to be initiated into the winter by two Canadian backwoodsmen who had spent thirty years traveling across the wilderness on snowshoes and by dogsled.

We planned to cross the entire Quebec-Labrador peninsula, spending a month traveling through the taiga and

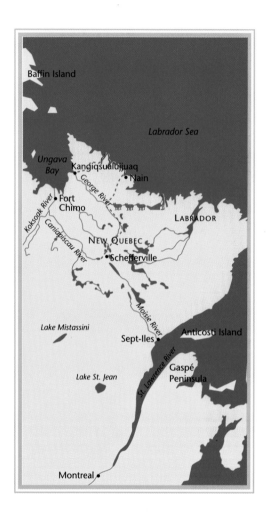

the tundra, followed by another month on the coastal ice before we climbed into the Torngatt Mountains to reach Kangiqsualujjuaq on Ungava Bay. It would be an extraordinary winter, during which we lived the harsh but exalting life of old-time frontiersmen.

Our equipment was made of traditional materials—leather, canvas, wood, and fur. For one thing, no synthetic materials are better adapted to travel in the wilderness. But also, our equipment was a pleasure to look at, being in harmony with the landscape. What could blend better with the colors of the taiga than a sled made entirely of wood and rawhide?

At night our canvas tent, heated by a small metal stove, provided us an island of warmth no bigger than a few square inches in the middle of the frozen wastes. In it we dried our clothes and cooked our one meal of the day.

It was primitive. But it was straight out of Jack London, and I was the happiest man in the world.

Hitching and Driving a Dogsled

People tend to think that it's easy to drive a dogsled. Far from it! It is a real sport, requiring strength, balance, and stamina.

If you're traveling off-trail you rarely spend much time standing on the runners.

You're either ahead of the sled breaking a trail through the deep snow with your snowshoes or behind it guiding it along or pushing.

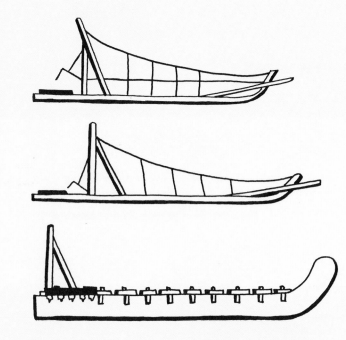

Right (top to bottom): There are three main types of dogsleds: the basket sled for use on marked trails, the toboggan sled for deep snow, and the Inuit sled for traveling over sea ice.

Driving and Turns

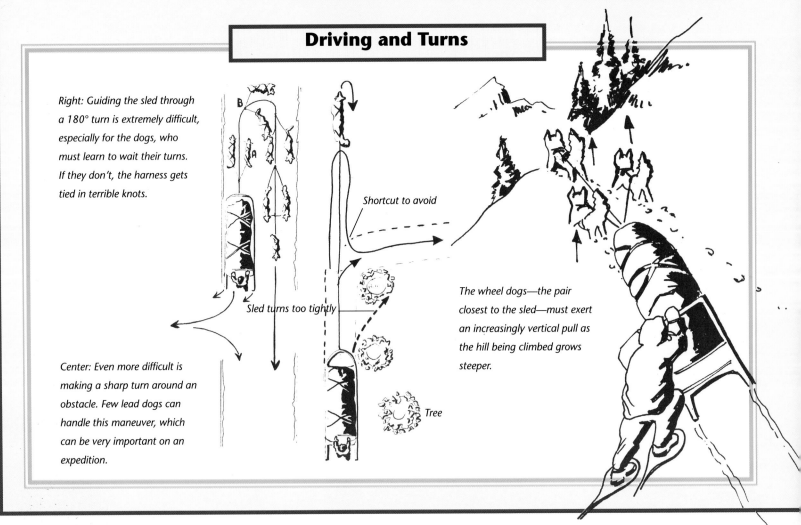

Right: Guiding the sled through a 180° turn is extremely difficult, especially for the dogs, who must learn to wait their turns. If they don't, the harness gets tied in terrible knots.

Center: Even more difficult is making a sharp turn around an obstacle. Few lead dogs can handle this maneuver, which can be very important on an expedition.

Shortcut to avoid

Sled turns too tightly

Tree

The wheel dogs—the pair closest to the sled—must exert an increasingly vertical pull as the hill being climbed grows steeper.

The Gee Pole Method

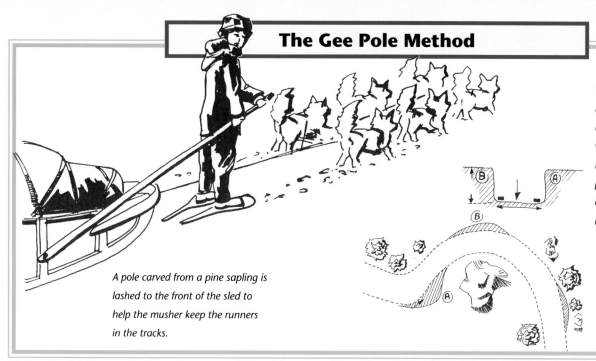

The gee pole becomes an absolute necessity on difficult terrain, particularly when the sled is heavily loaded. Without the gee pole, the sled would slew off into areas of deep snow (A and B).

A pole carved from a pine sapling is lashed to the front of the sled to help the musher keep the runners in the tracks.

Harness Configurations

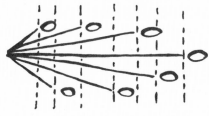

Lines correspond to ropes; ovals represent dogs.

Top: A single-tandem hitch is used by some woodland Indians.

Center: The double-tandem hitch is the most common.

Below: The fan hitch is used by the Inuit for traveling over sea ice.

The surface of coastal sea ice is often ideal for covering great distances.

The lashings for dogsleds are made of natural materials more and more rarely. This is unfortunate. Natural materials are more attractive, more in keeping with the landscape, and also more practical—wood and rawhide are much easier to find in the wilderness than carbon fiber.

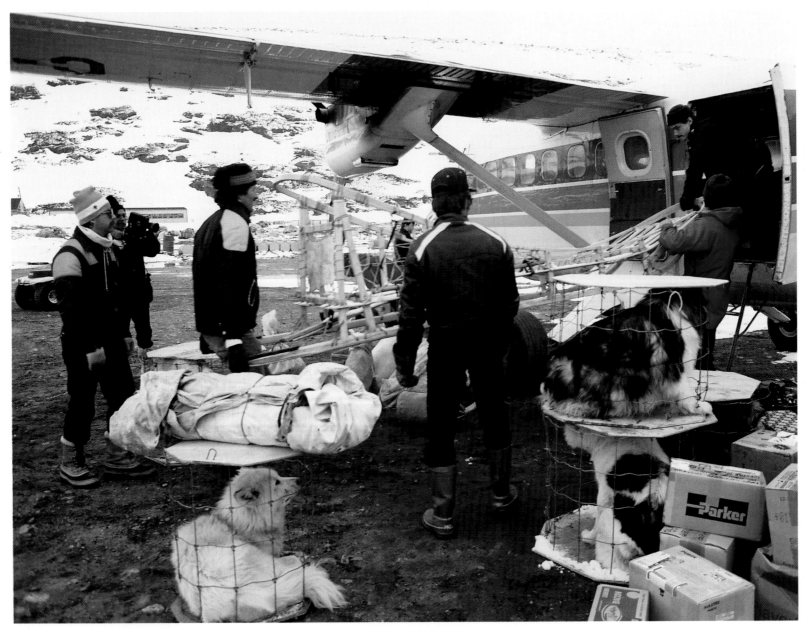

An expedition to the Far North often requires a great deal of planning. Dogs and equipment have to be flown in, which is a complex and expensive operation.

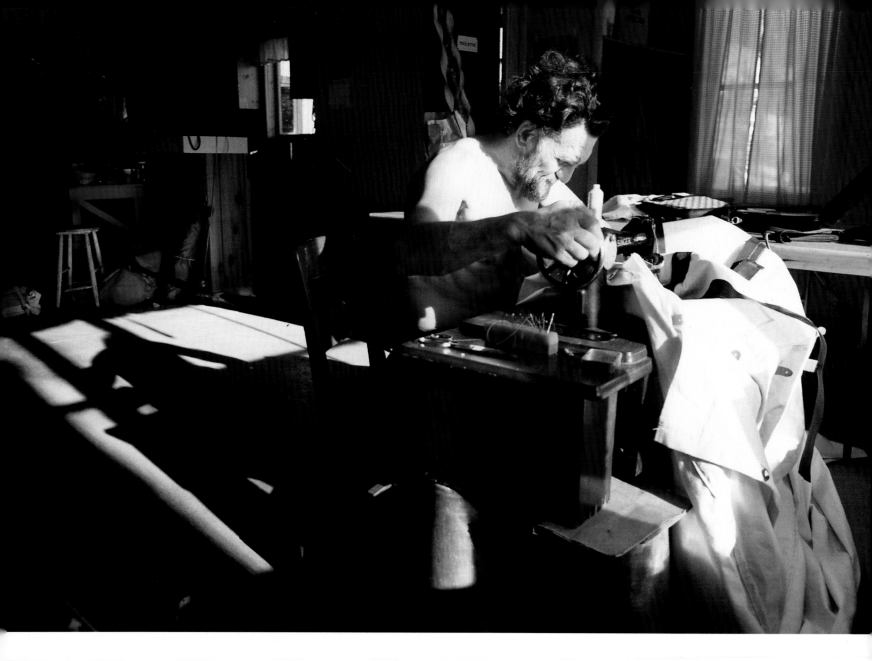

For our crossing of the Quebec-Labrador peninsula, Jacques Duhoux, one of two experienced backwoodsmen on our team, devised a conical tent like a teepee. Not only did it offer less wind resistance, but it had the advantage of having only one tent pole, in the center.

We are not trying to be heroes. We are simply travelers who are drawn to wide-open spaces, which fascinate and beguile us.

My life was linked
to the Far North
the way a man's
destiny may be
joined to a woman's
from the moment
their eyes meet.

*In the mountainous region of extreme
northern Labrador, the only flat ground we
could find for a campsite was on a frozen
lake. Ice conducts the cold, unlike snow, and
this caused us some discomfort. But there
were also advantages. By digging down six
feet through the ice we were able to have an
indoor sink. This was the only time we ever
had the luxury of running water in our tent!*

The Wind-Chill Factor

Crossing a fjord in Labrador.

Wind chill is the cooling effect of the wind at a given temperature as measured in terms of the loss of body heat. The highest risk of frostbite does not occur at the lowest temperatures. The human body tolerates –40° F in windless conditions better than 0° F with a 25 mph wind (which is equivalent to a temperature of –55° F). During a blizzard—with such a storm's high winds—it is possible to experience a theoretical temperature of –110° F. Going out in such weather, even for very short periods, requires the very greatest precautions.

Opposite: We were not always able to travel over the sea, since it was only partially frozen. We therefore had to make long detours along the jagged Labrador coastline. Men and dogs often had to pull together to make it up the steeper slopes.

During our dogsled expedition, we covered about a thousand miles in less than three months and encountered varied terrain— taiga (right), tundra, sea ice, and mountains.

Men wanted for Hazardous Journey.
Small wages, bitter cold, long
months of complete darkness,
constant danger, safe return
doubtful. Honour and recognition
in case of success.

**Advertisement placed in a London newspaper by Sir Ernest Shackleton,
who received many applications**

The dogs after a blizzard.

Sleeping in –60° F weather is not pleasant. Your breath freezes immediately on contact with the cold air and forms a crust of ice that has to be wiped off every half hour. Though you wake up all the time at temperatures below –40° F, your sleep is deep and efficient. In such extreme conditions, you realize that there is nothing particularly natural about sleeping eight hours straight.

Opposite: The aurora borealis unfurls its ribbons of light in the sky over Labrador.

The Hudson's Bay Company

In the seventeenth century, the demand for furs was so great that white men traveled everywhere in search of them, often threatening the local ecology and peoples. Among the most daring traders and explorers in New France was Pierre Esprit Radisson, who had an extraordinary knowledge of the region. On his return from a long and difficult expedition to Hudson Bay in 1665, he was discouraged by the French lack of interest and approached the English. Vast resources, as well as a passage to the East, were to be had in the north. On May 2, 1670, English King Charles II granted a charter to "the Governor and Company of Adventurers of England trading into Hudson's Bay," better known as the Hudson's Bay Company, or, as it is called today, the Bay.

In 1739, once French-English territorial disputes were settled, the trading posts in Hudson Bay sent to London 69,911 beaver pelts, the furs of 15,196 martens, 355 otters, 1,011 lynxes, 853 wolverines, 266 bears, and 454 wolves, and the hides of 76 moose and 14 deer.

The North West Company, a rival of the Hudson's Bay Company since the late eighteenth century, finally merged with it in 1821. Owning or managing half of the territory of Canada from the Atlantic to the Pacific, the monopoly at one time wielded phenomenal power. In 1869, the company sold this kingdom—which measured thirty-three times the size of England—to the newly formed Dominion of Canada for the sum of 300,000 pounds.

Inuit women's parkas are equipped with a large pouch in the back, in which they carry their babies.

It is glorious to see the herds of caribou coming from the forests and starting their migration north.

Timidly they look for the traps set by men.

It is glorious to see the great herds emerging from the forests and spreading over the white plains.

It is glorious to see.

It is glorious to see the caribou with their long winter coats returning to the forests.

Fearfully they look for the little people while the herd follows the low-tide mark, their hooves striking against each other.

It is glorious when the time of the migrations arrives.

Inuit song

The Inuit

Inuit means "human beings." When the first white explorers arrived, they seized on the Algonquin-Cree word *askimon,* an insult meaning "eaters of raw meat," and applied it to the native peoples of the north, calling them *Eskimo.* But the term *Inuit,* the name they apply to themselves, is the one preferred today in most areas (the singular form is *Inuk*). The Inuit originated in Asia some five thousand years ago and dispersed across the Arctic over a land bridge then joining Asia and North America at the Bering Strait. The Inuit world, which extends over more than four thousand miles, can be divided into three major areas:

- To the west, the Alaskan coast, peopled in part by the Aleuts. The more southern of them built dwellings of wood and whalebone, while the more northern excavated huts half underground.
- To the east, Greenland, where the Inuit often lived in stone structures. Like Inuit elsewhere, they used igloos in winter when traveling.
- The central region, in Canada from the Mackenzie River in the Northwest Territories to Labrador. These Inuit have faced a constant struggle to survive against the hardships of a hostile environment.

Only the older Inuit women still know how to make waterproof sealskin boots, or mukluks, which are ideal for walking over the ice pack in spring.

Sealskin Boots

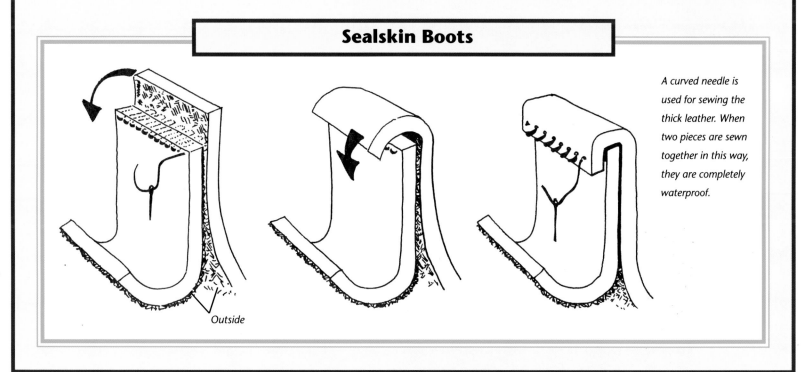

Outside

A curved needle is used for sewing the thick leather. When two pieces are sewn together in this way, they are completely waterproof.

The cold is like a vicious dog
that must be tamed or it will bite.

When you find wood to heat the tent at night, the first things you dry are your footwear and hats, which get wet from perspiration and breathing.

It is here on the sea ice that Mahingan, our lead dog, gave birth to two pups. We had put her in a sleeping bag in the front of the sled and found that evening that our party included two more dogs.

The surface of the sea does not freeze easily. Salt can bring the freezing point as low as 14° F, and the wind and tides constantly break up the ice as it forms.

North and South Poles

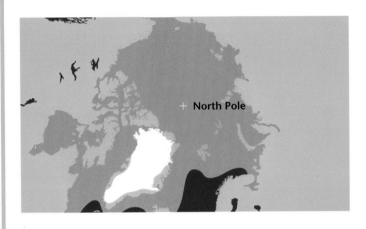

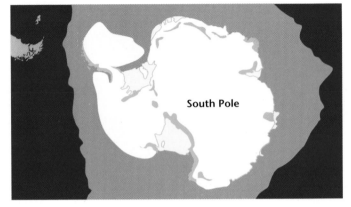

The North Pole has no fixed position; it is a constantly moving spot on the frozen ocean.

The North Pole is much warmer than the South Pole, where temperatures in the range of −90° to −110° F are often recorded in winter.

Coastal Ice

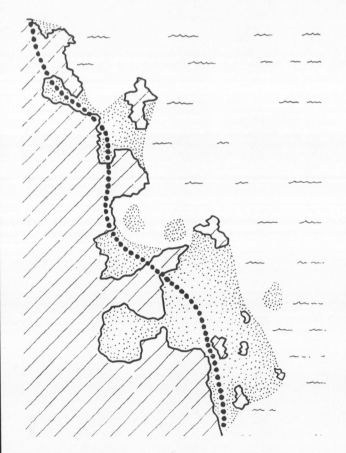

When traveling by dogsled along a coast, the best route to follow can be determined from the charts. In theory, any stretch of sea ice not anchored by islands is to be avoided.

 Open sea

 Mainland or island

 Sea ice

•••••••• Dogsled route

The term "pack ice" refers to any ice surface formed at sea. Depending on the salt content of the water, the ice may freeze at temperatures as low as 14° to 28° F. In the first stages, crystals form, which gives the sea an almost oily appearance—this is frazil ice. Then plates of ice appear and gradually weld together. The wind, tides, and swell break these plates up a hundred times before they freeze for good. Then the salt starts to concentrate in "brine pockets," from which it eventually escapes, dragged down by its own weight, and so, little by little, the ice loses its salinity. After a few months, the pack may freeze to a depth of sixteen feet, but the channels and water-ways cutting across it still give it a certain amount of mobility.

The thousands of miles of ice pack help determine the climate by considerably reducing the exchanges that would otherwise occur between the unfrozen ocean and the atmosphere. The ice surface reflects more than 80 percent of the sun's energy back into space, as opposed to the 20 percent that is reflected off the surface of the ocean. This accounts for a very significant reduction in heat in the region.

Overflow: Even in the dead of winter, water can rise onto the surface of the ice and mix with snow. The result is slush.

In winter, the ice pack captures icebergs.

Because they speak the same language, Quebecois are often taken for Frenchmen, but this is a mistake—their mindset is entirely different. Michel Denis and Jacques Duhoux, two seasoned backwoodsmen, proved to us during the trip that the old ways of the frontier easily outstripped the new technologies.

The Inuit, once scattered along the whole coast of Labrador, have now gathered in the town of Nain, the only settlement on the coast.

The Baby Seal Affair

Any mention of seals in the Far North is bound to trigger images from the international campaign waged to protect the lives of harp seal pups. The pictures did their work; everyone remembers the shots of those adorable little balls of fur being clubbed and then falling bloody to the ice. Meanwhile, few people seem to care about the Inuits, who once survived by hunting what is, to be sure, a very photogenic animal.

In 1977, a number of activist groups raised an outcry against the hunting of seal pups, supporting their arguments with grisly images of baby seals being clubbed to death by hunters. As a result, buying and selling seal fur is no longer allowed. The seal populations have increased dramatically, to the point where in some areas seals face starvation and death. The ecological balance, which has always included Inuit hunters taking their share, has been destroyed. The social and economic consequences for the Inuit, who are now more dependent on government aid than ever, have also been severe. This was surely not the intended aim of the campaign. It would have been smarter to establish more humane ways of hunting seals and to show concern for the people who derived their livelihood from hunting, rather than spend vast amounts on exhibiting grisly images.

The cute little thing with its big eyes calling for help, and the brute with his club. Maybe this version of the story is a little too simplistic.

Seal Hunting

Seal meat and blubber are excellent foods for sled dogs, but hunting for seals requires a great deal of experience and, above all, patience. Since seals are constantly being hunted by polar bears, they are very wary.

To approach a seal, the hunter crouches behind a piece of white cloth, moving only during the few seconds when the seal is not looking. The process can take several hours.

If the seal isn't killed on the first shot, it'll escape back to the sea through its breathing hole. Seals make their own breathing holes and keep them open through the winter.

With a String of Twelve Packhorses in the Rocky Mountains

IN THE FILM *Jeremiah Johnson*, there is a moment when the trapper, standing on the crest of a high mountain, realizes that he could go either north or south, but it wouldn't make any difference. "I'm free," he says, "and the Rockies are a big, wild land." As I was watching the movie, I decided that I, too, would travel to the Rockies one day.

With two expeditions behind me—a summer canoe trip and a winter dogsled journey—I felt I wanted to experience the succession of the seasons in the field. I would live in the mountains for a year or more, using whatever transportation was appropriate to the season and terrain, traveling through the Rocky Mountains from Wyoming to Alaska, a distance of 4,300 miles, along the wilderness valleys of Montana, Alberta, British Columbia, and the Yukon. It would take a year—with a twelve-horse pack string in the warm-weather months and with two teams of sled dogs when there was snow.

Looking at the map on which I had drawn our itinerary, I felt the line

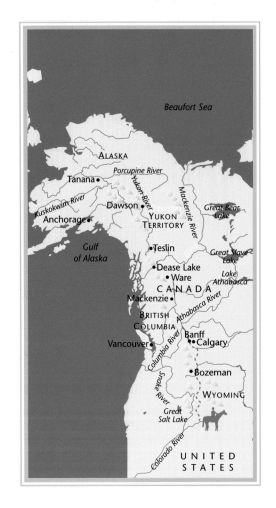

was somehow incomplete, as though it were a figure that was missing a head or a leg. The line stopped on the Alaska border for no logical reason. We would be there in the spring. Why not wait there until the breakup and go down the Yukon by raft like the Klondike gold rushers who had pioneered that country? Then we could cross the Alaska Range (which includes Denali), join the headwaters of the Kuskokwim River, and follow it down to the Bering Sea.

I traced that route on the map and the line came to an end neatly at the water's edge. This was much better. The journey would now take a year and a half, or more. It made no difference; I'd still pack the same things.

A year of hard work was required to raise the funds for this "triple expedition" and to make the necessary preparations for the three preliminary phases: training the dogs, choosing the expedition members, and assembling the equipment—not to mention reconnaissance trips and conditioning in the Rockies.

But once the machine was set in motion . . .

How can you buy and sell the sky, heat, the earth?

The idea is strange to us. We do not own the freshness of the air

or the reflection on the water; how then can you buy them from us?

We know that the white man does not understand our ways.

The white man is a stranger who takes from the earth what he needs.

The earth is not his brother but his enemy.

When he has conquered it he moves on. Yet the earth does not belong

to man. Man belongs to the earth, and all things share

the same breath: animals, men, and trees. The white man's appetite

will devour the earth and leave nothing but a desert.

From an 1854 letter from Chief Seattle to President Franklin Pierce, on the proposed sale of Indian lands

Above: A Sekani Indian in a motorboat. Traveling upstream, it takes him only a few hours to cover the distance it took his ancestors several days to paddle.

My father in Alberta. He taught me to fish when I was five. When he was fifty I introduced him to the Far North.

Rivers are the biggest obstacle when traveling on horseback. Finding a usable ford often means making long detours.

Fishing in Fast Rivers

You don't become a river fisherman by improvising. The fish are in very specific locations, and you may go hungry unless you know where they are.

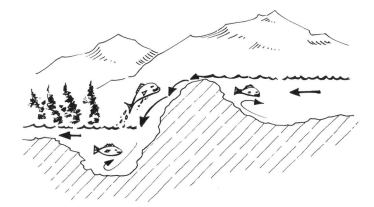

Predatory fish like trout and salmon lie in wait for their prey.

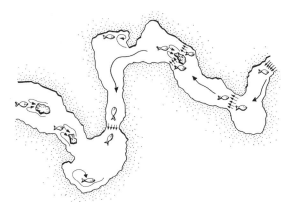

Fish can be found in places where the currents cancel each other out and where they can maintain their position with a minimum of exertion.

Sacajawea

Without her help, Lewis and Clark would never have succeeded in crossing the continent.

Sacajawea was a Shoshone Indian who guided Meriwether Lewis and William Clark through Montana's labyrinth of mountains, dead-end valleys, and ravines for the first crossing of the Rockies by U.S. citizens. The mission of their historic expedition was to explore the Louisiana Purchase and the land beyond. They reached the continental divide in the Bitterroot Mountains on April 12, 1805, and descended the far side in animal-hide rafts, on rivers filled with rapids and shallows. Later, American explorer Robert Stuart discovered an easier crossing, the South Pass, which became more widely used.

The most tedious job when horse packing is loading and unloading the horses, which takes more than three hours a day.

You can still find huge herds of cattle driven by
one or two men in the high valleys of Wyoming.
We played cowboy for a day and helped a
wrangler round up his livestock.

We always chose our campsites with great care in order to enjoy the spectacular views the Rockies offer wherever there is a slight clearing. The menu for the evening meal depended on what fish or game we had caught. Left: Venison à la carte.

A Winter Camp

For a century, backwoodsmen, trappers, and prospectors have used a traditional canvas tent. They bring a woodstove into the tent as soon as the first frost has occurred. Made of light galvanized metal, it is used both for cooking and drying out equipment. In the wintertime, the stove becomes indispensable.

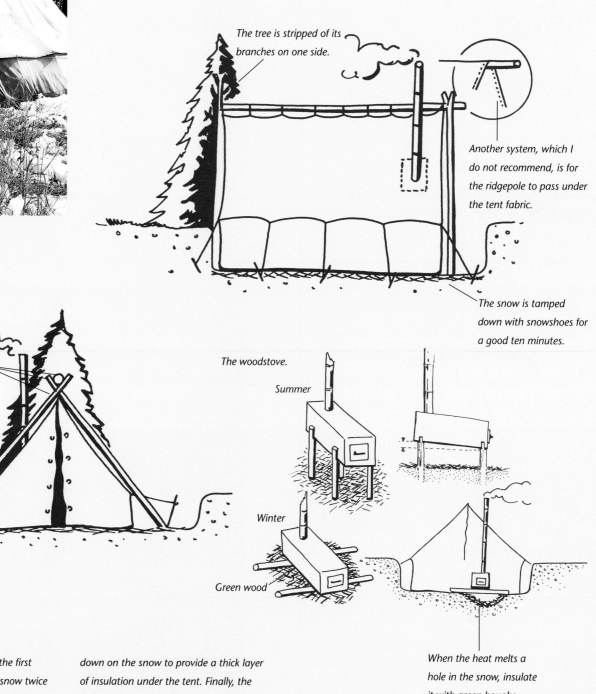

The tree is stripped of its branches on one side.

Another system, which I do not recommend, is for the ridgepole to pass under the tent fabric.

The snow is tamped down with snowshoes for a good ten minutes.

Three stripped trunks provide support for the tent.

The woodstove.

Summer

Winter

Green wood

When the heat melts a hole in the snow, insulate it with green boughs.

When pitching a tent in winter, the first step is to pack down an area of snow twice the size of the tent with your snowshoes. Then three slender conifers are felled and their branches are stripped off and laid down on the snow to provide a thick layer of insulation under the tent. Finally, the three trunks are used to support the tent. The ridgepole is usually supported at one end by a tree.

Wyoming

Bayard Fox, a realer-than-life cowboy with a Colt strapped to his belt and legs bowed from long years of riding, had rounded up 250 horses for us in a corral. We were to choose the twelve we wanted to use. It was a test of sorts. Luckily we had an expert on our team, Paul Perrier, who had spent fifty of his sixty-four years working horses—and he wasn't going to be taken in easily. He walked into the corral and, under the baking Wyoming sun, picked out fifteen horses over the next two hours. Bayard Fox watched, a grass stem between his teeth, judging the man judging the horses. Paul passed the test with flying colors. Bayard agreed with ten of Paul's choices, and went back to the corral for two more. Paul, in turn, approved of Bayard's decision, exclaiming, "Strong horses—good for the Rockies!"

Then we had to learn to pack loads on the horses, which was no easy task. The pack saddles have to be cinched on just right, neither too loose nor too tight, and since the horses swell out their bellies as soon as a saddle touches their backs, this was a challenge. Then the load has to be balanced before being covered with a tarp. The last step is tying the diamond hitch that holds the whole thing together.

At first, our dream of a wild ride in the mountains was more like a nightmare. The horses would break loose, and, badly loaded, would strew equipment over miles and miles of rugged landscape. They got sores, which meant that we had to walk for days without once getting into the saddle. And to top it all, we went for a week without catching a fish or shooting a bird to eat.

After a hundred miles, though, we were broken to the trail and by the time we met up again with Bayard Fox, six hundred miles on, we were pleased to hear him sing out, "Well done, men! You are the best packers!"

When Punkie took a heart-stopping fall of six or seven hundred feet down a rocky slope, we expected to find him broken into pieces, but other than suffering a few cuts he was miraculously unhurt.

Packing Loads on a Horse

There are many ways to load a packhorse, and every region has its favorite. In Wyoming, they use a diamond hitch.

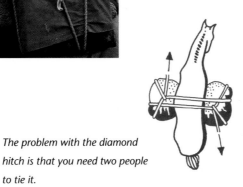

The problem with the diamond hitch is that you need two people to tie it.

The girth has to be positioned carefully to make sure the rope does not come in contact with the horse's skin.

What's impressive about the Rockies is not the number of animals it harbors but their great variety.

This region is home to such high-altitude animals as mountain goat and bighorn sheep, and members of the deer family—mule deer (left), white-tailed deer, elk, moose (the largest member of the deer family), and caribou—which live in valleys and alpine meadows, usually in herds.

Grizzly and black bears, as well as wolves, lynx, and mountain lions, also inhabit the Rockies. A full list of all the wildlife of the region would be much longer; these are only the large mammals.

The Bighorn Sheep, Lord of the High Mountains

This mountain climber, a symbol of the Rocky Mountains, lives at high altitudes, usually on inaccessible ridges. The Indians of the Yellowstone region were once its heaviest predator. Though reduced in number now and restricted to a much narrower range, bighorn sheep nonetheless prosper in their high mountain habitat. The rams usually live alone. They join the herd during the rutting season, in December, when they clash in fierce butting contests, but by January they retake their solitary heights.

As long as the snow is no more than a foot and a half deep and the temperature stays above −20° F, a pack string can still travel. Above: In Alberta in October.

Writer and filmmaker Alain Rastoin accompanied us on our first big expeditions. Knowing how to ride a horse or drive a dogsled is not enough to make someone a good team member. An expedition also needs people who are good organizers and fundraisers, and Alain was highly capable in these areas.

Advancing with twelve horses along a six-foot ledge on an exposed mountainside requires enormous care. One night we almost found ourselves stopped here at an altitude of ten thousand feet by a blizzard.

Mountains are to the rest of
the body of the earth,
what violent muscular action
is to the body of man.

John Ruskin

What use are our dreams,

unless we sometimes

make them come true?

Pack and Saddle Horses

On a long-distance horse-packing expedition, there's an old saying that can't be repeated too often: "If you plan to travel far, take good care of your horse." At night, you have to find good grazing for the horses, of course, but you also have to keep them from straying.

Thin rope that will break under excess strain.

The peg is screwed into the ground in the middle of a grassy area. The tether should be thirty or forty feet long.

Well-trained packhorses will follow without being tied.

Long hand-held lead.

5 feet

Hobble used by the Tofalar.

American-style hobble.

Once off the beaten trail, a packhorse expedition is a great deal like a dogsled trip—you spend a lot more time on foot than in the saddle. At high elevations, such as here in Montana above 11,500 feet, the ground is hidden by snow, making progress slow and hazardous. We walk in front of the horses to pick the best route, and also to act as brakes.

Dogsledding in the Canadian Rockies

IMAGINE the following scene. Twenty sled dogs and four men have just landed in the heart of the Rocky Mountains, after having crossed the Atlantic by plane and Canada by truck (a total distance of 3,700 miles!). They are there to undertake a three-month journey to Alaska.

But the temperature on that mid-January day is an unseasonable 34° F! Nothing comparable had ever been seen. Meanwhile, back in the Jura Mountains of France, where the dogs had been training, the temperature registered −10° F! The whole world was topsy-turvy. We all felt our spirits plummet as the mercury rose. The rivers opened, and the ice broke—catastrophe.

Everyone advised us not to go. But off we went. A Sekani Indian, setting little store by our obstinacy, offered us a bracelet of considerable sentimental value: "Take it. If you get through, keep

it! Otherwise return it to me when you come back, which will be very soon."

Actually, we did not turn back, but our crossing of the Cassiar Mountains north of Dease Lake in northern British Columbia took nine weeks instead of the three we'd planned. Since we had brought enough food for only four weeks, we hunted to survive. We were forced to grind it out in the forests and mountains in order to avoid the open rivers, where we risked our skins more than once.

Breaking trail on snowshoes and chopping down trees with an ax, we sometimes traveled no more than three miles a day. And then we still had to catch our dinner, which meant following the trail of a moose or caribou to the last hoofprint, the one with the hoof still in it. But we hung on, and the dogs did, too. We kept the bracelet, and its owner became our friend.

The Breakup of a River

In the winter wilds, rivers are the only roads. Once the coldest part of the winter is past, the threat of breakup is always present—and if it comes when the sled teams are still far from anywhere, it can spell disaster.

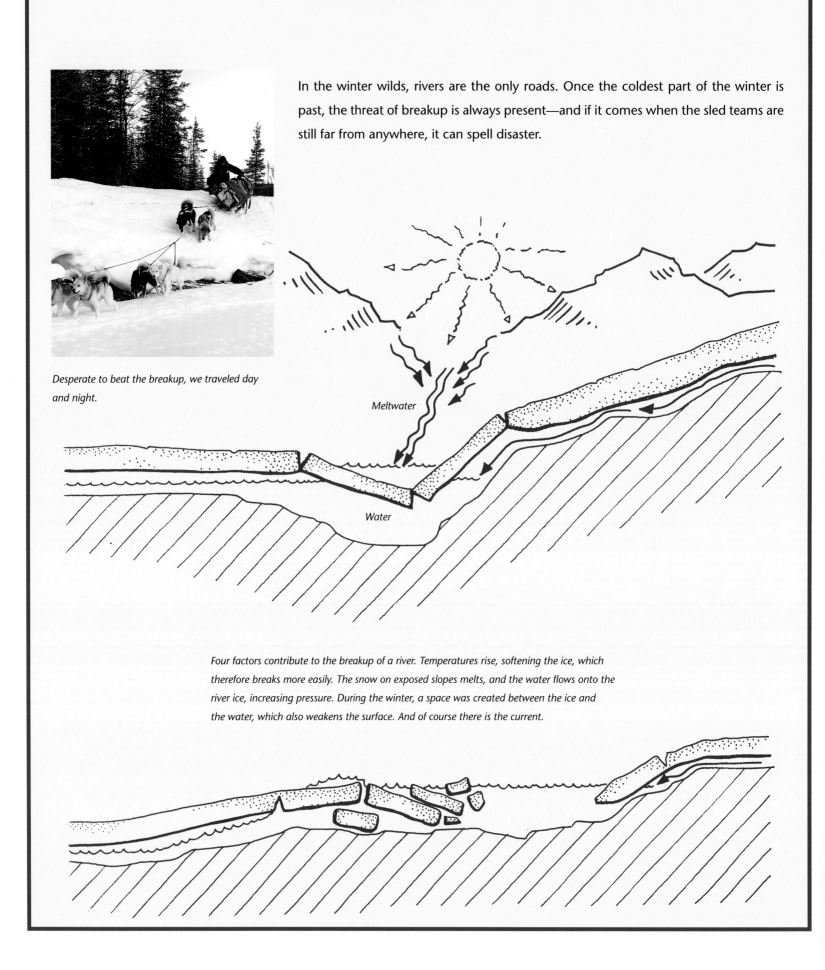

Desperate to beat the breakup, we traveled day and night.

Meltwater

Water

Four factors contribute to the breakup of a river. Temperatures rise, softening the ice, which therefore breaks more easily. The snow on exposed slopes melts, and the water flows onto the river ice, increasing pressure. During the winter, a space was created between the ice and the water, which also weakens the surface. And of course there is the current.

In some cases the snow is so deep that even with snowshoes it cannot be packed down enough for the dogs and sled to pass over it. Progress then becomes extremely difficult.

A porcupine is a ball of needles. When approached by a dog, the porcupine whips its tail around, sending quills into the dog's face. If they are not removed quickly, the dog will die.

In the depths of winter, some swift-moving portions of a river stay open. The ice that forms there breaks and is compressed into an ice pack that is difficult to cross. Deep snow presents another hardship when you're traveling off-trail. Both men and dogs find it exhausting to drag a sled weighing more than five hundred pounds through powder.

When the snow is very deep, a heavily loaded sled always tends to sink, first to one side then the other. It is important to keep it as level as possible.

When sled dogs are working hard, they need a daily ration of five to ten pounds of meat. Between our two teams, this came to over two hundred pounds a day. A moose, yielding four hundred to six hundred pounds of meat, was ideal for our purposes, especially when we could kill one near the camp. The dogs can be let loose on the carcass. Otherwise, it has to be cut up and the meat brought back to camp (opposite).

Whence comes the strange attraction of the polar regions, so strong and so tenacious that a man forgets the mental and physical fatigue they have caused him and longs only to return there?

French explorer Jean-Baptiste Charcot

Louis Bavière, who was originally fascinated by wolves, became the first Frenchman to own a team of Greenland huskies. He and I were linked by a deep understanding. With his dreamer-philosopher's temperament, he brought a new perspective to the Far North.

The Greenland husky is a pure sled dog, having been bred for centuries by the greatest snow-country travelers on the planet, the Inuit.

Deep in the forest a call was sounding,

and as often as he heard this call,

mysteriously thrilling and luring, he felt

compelled to turn his back upon the fire

and the beaten earth around it, and to

plunge into the forest, and on and on,

he knew not where or why.

Jack London, *The Call of the Wild*

On the Gold Rush Trail

THE MYTHIC CITY of Dawson, at the confluence of the Yukon and Klondike rivers, was founded during the great Klondike gold rush, which spawned the legends of *White Fang* and *The Call of the Wild*. You can still visit Jack London's cabin there, and the bars still accept gold dust in payment for whiskey. All the buildings are made of wood, and adventure calls on every street corner. This city under the midnight sun has a big soul and enormous charm, to which we willingly fell victim. Our plan was to make camp a short way upstream from the city, build a raft—a carbon copy of the ones used by nineteenth-century gold rushers—and float down the Yukon River to its confluence with the Tanana. We thought it would take about two weeks to build our raft, but we hadn't reckoned on the way things work in Dawson. We ended up staying there more than a month. But at least we remained true to our motto, which had always been "Time wasted on the trail is time well spent."

Later we made up for lost time by rafting downriver around the clock, traveling 120 miles per day, stopping only once in a while to take on

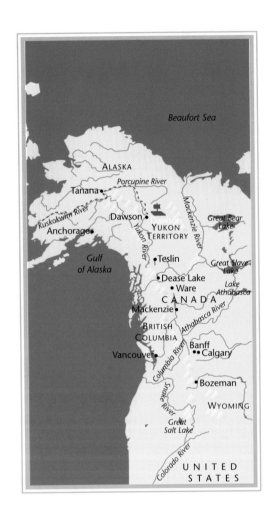

firewood and clean water or to go exploring on a mountain. The crew of the raft was divided into ship's watches, with two men taking turns at the helm while the other three slept, ate, fished, or daydreamed on deck. Occasionally we would all have to row together to bring the raft back to the middle of the current or avoid shallows or a rock. We did this with the help of large oars placed at either end of the *Coulapic*, as we had baptized our raft in Dawson (it means "Sinks-like-a-stone" in French). This was an easy passage, different in every way from the one that lay ahead.

For two weeks we floated with the current, but now we would have to fight against it to cross from the Yukon watershed into the Kuskokwim's. To do this, we crossed the border and set off in canoes into the no-man's-land of Alaska. For more than a month we saw no sign of a human—only bear, caribou, moose, beaver, and other wildlife. Wolves stood on the banks and watched us pass, and we in turn watched them in the long evenings chase young geese in the swamps. It took us six weeks to paddle, line, and portage our canoes mile by mile against the current to our goal.

The Raft, Adrift on the Current

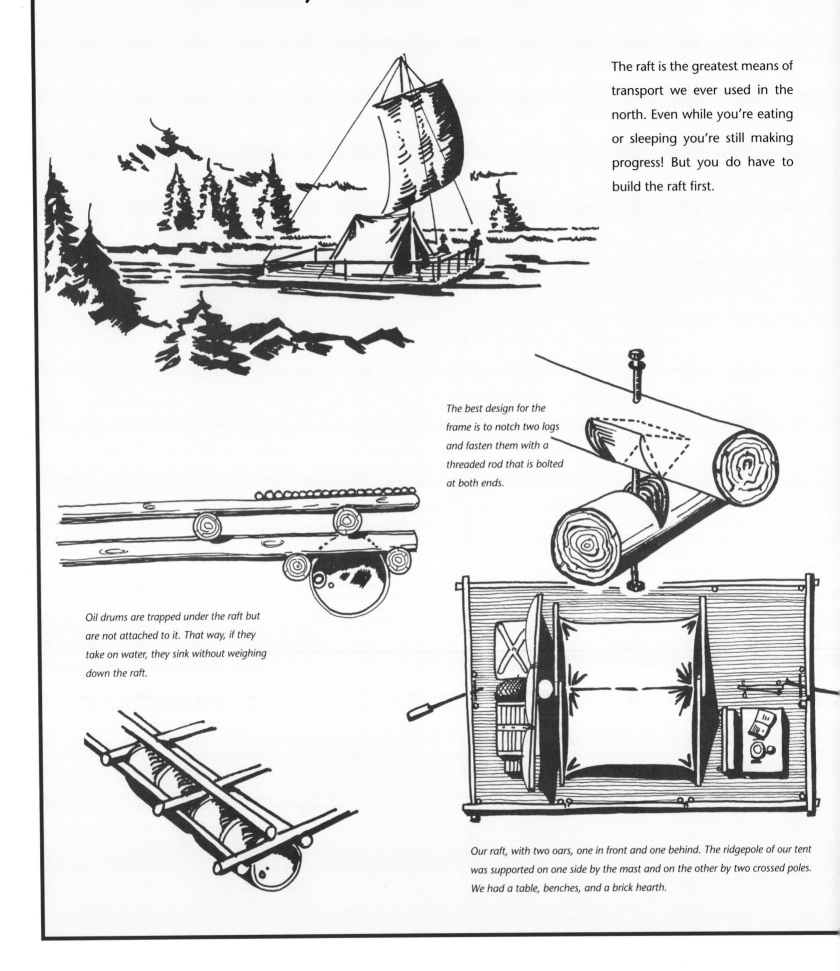

The raft is the greatest means of transport we ever used in the north. Even while you're eating or sleeping you're still making progress! But you do have to build the raft first.

The best design for the frame is to notch two logs and fasten them with a threaded rod that is bolted at both ends.

Oil drums are trapped under the raft but are not attached to it. That way, if they take on water, they sink without weighing down the raft.

Our raft, with two oars, one in front and one behind. The ridgepole of our tent was supported on one side by the mast and on the other by two crossed poles. We had a table, benches, and a brick hearth.

Building the Raft

If we had to build another raft, there is little we would change except the size. Ours, measuring some 650 square feet, weighed several tons, and proved hard to handle in rapids and shallows.

The bark should be removed as soon as the tree is felled and before the sap dries. Before you put the logs together, it is best to wait forty-eight hours, so their surface will be dry.

Be sure to build the raft in a place from which you'll be able to launch it later!

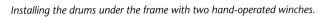
Installing the drums under the frame with two hand-operated winches.

In the Yukon Flats, a shallow section of the river with many islands, blind sloughs, and sandbanks, the men on watch always try to keep the raft in the center of the main current.

This was an easy passage, different in every way from the one that lay ahead.

I have crossed Labrador, Alaska, and Siberia with André Michalclak, alias "Totoche." On an expedition he always seeks encounters with nature, of course, but also with other human beings.

Opposite: Several times our raft drifted out of the main current and became grounded on a sandbar. We would then have to tow it, sometimes for hours, until we could bring it back into the deep waters of the river's main channel.

There is no better way to preserve meat and keep the flies away than to smoke and dry it (above left). Partridges are eaten immediately, as are rabbits and ducks (above right).

The Beaver, the Great Construction Engineer

Beavers were at the heart of the huge expansion in the fur trade at the end of the sixteenth century. Their history in some sense recapitulates the history of Canada, where beaver pelts once served as a basis for monetary exchange. The unit of currency was the pelu, equivalent to a beaver fur, and twenty-five pelus could buy a gun.

Building a Dam

Above: The dam looks like a waterproof mat tipped at a 45° angle and is supported by log pilings that straighten as the dam rises.

Beavers bend every which way to bring down the bigger trees using their sharp teeth (below right: upper and lower incisors).

Below: The waterproof mat is coated with liquid mud from the bottom of the stream or lake.

 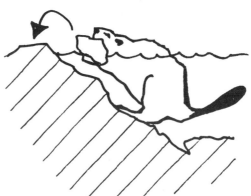 

Beaver Houses

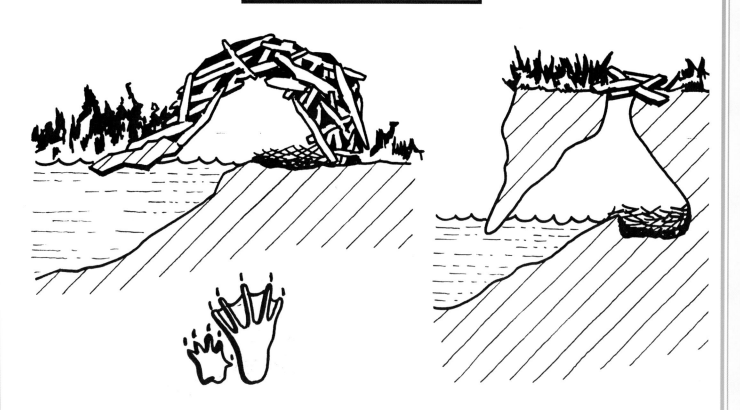

Beavers build two kinds of shelters: the beaver lodge, made of mud and branches (above left), and a sort of large den that they tunnel into the bank (above right). Above: Beaver pawprints, front and back.

Beavers cut down small trees growing on the shore and stick them into the river bottom in front of their lodges to cache food for the winter.

There are three ways of going upriver in a canoe: paddling, which works as long as the current is slower than 5 mph; lining (illustrated above), when the terrain and vegetation of the bank allow it; and poling, which the Indians once practiced extensively, and which requires a great deal of expertise.

Alaska

The territory once belonged to Russia, which sold it in March 1867 to the United States for $7.2 million, a pittance.

After the gold rush, which lasted until the early 1900s (and the international success of Jack London's novels), Alaska became strategically important in containing the Russian giant. The gold gone, Alaska saw an oil boom, and a pipeline was built across eight hundred miles of country from Prudhoe Bay to the port of Valdez, where the black gold is loaded onto tankers.

At night around the fire, we ate and talked about what we missed most—a good meal, our families, women. . . .

While creating the world,
God suddenly felt very tired.
When he got to the last
wheelbarrowful, he decided
just to dump it anywhere,
and this is how Alaska
came into being.

Alaskan folktale

Fishing on an Expedition

In Alaska, when the water is clear and the spot well chosen, it can take only a few minutes to catch the evening meal.

You tend to fish more from necessity than for pleasure on an expedition. But whatever the reason to fish, you should do it in the right place, at the right time, and with the right equipment. Results can be stunning, as fish tend to congregate in certain areas of a lake or river. One night, when two of us went line fishing, we brought in more than half a ton of trout, each fish weighing between two and twenty pounds!

Trout, pike, and salmon are the fish most commonly found in the northlands. One also finds char, grayling, pike, and whitefish, as well as catfish and amur in Russia.

Good Knots for Fishing

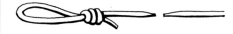

The line breaks: an excellent knot.

A bad knot: the knot breaks.

Another bad knot: the line breaks at the base of the knot.

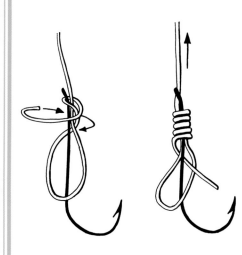

There is nothing more infuriating than losing a splendid fish after several hours of walking and patient fishing, all because of a badly tied knot. Some knots constrict the line, making it quick to break. It's good to avoid such knots and use reliable ones such as these instead.

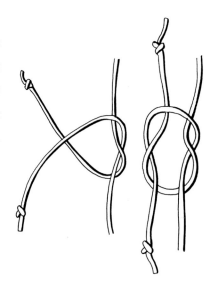

From Mongolia to Irkutsk with the Tofalar and a String of Twelve Horses

"IMPOSSIBLE. Permissions are not granted for what you want to do." The Soviet ambassador in Paris was categorical in his refusal. Although perestroika was in the air, these were still the days when travelers supplied the authorities with a statement of their trip's purpose, the names of the hotels they would stay at, and a list of the people they were likely to meet. Ninety-five percent of the territory I planned to travel through was off-limits to foreigners. Even requesting a high-ranking KGB officer as an escort, I had only one chance in a thousand of carrying out even a quarter of my plan—to cross Siberia under my own steam from Mongolia to the Arctic Sea.

As he stood up to shake my hand, the ambassador joked: "The only person who could possibly help you is Mikhail Gorbachev!" And who could contact the president of the USSR on our behalf if not his French counter-

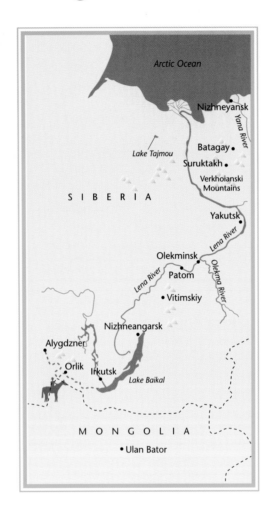

part, François Mitterrand? I had hunted boar one day with one of Mitterrand's best friends. I drove down to his country house to explain the whole situation. He demurred, as I had expected, refusing to trade on his friendship on behalf of anyone. In the end, Mitterrand did help me out, at least indirectly, but it was more that I helped myself. After a year of sleepless nights, of shuttling back and forth between Moscow and Paris, of writing hundreds of letters and brooking countless disappointments, I finally found myself about to set off.

Then I was blackmailed by Russian authorities who told me to pay an enormous sum of money or I could not go.

I didn't pay, and I set off anyway. It was summertime. We started our Asian journey on horseback, as it was the only way to travel across the vast mountains between Mongolia and Lake Baikal.

The Buryat people live in southern Siberia around Lake Baikal. Primarily fishermen, they are also hunters, trappers, and herders, but the recent influx of hard currency from tourism has begun to disrupt their traditional way of life.

Opposite: In the Siberian taiga, bridges are rare. They serve no purpose in the winter—it's easy enough to cross on the ice itself—and the cost of building structures solid enough to withstand a river's breakup and flood stages is prohibitive. In summer, primitive ferries cross the river, and people, vehicles, and a variety of animals crowd on board together.

The Taiga

The taiga—an enormous swath of evergreens just south of the tundra—is the largest forest in the world. It covers 10 percent of the earth's surface and accounts for one-quarter of its forested land. The taiga extends roughly from the fifty-fifth parallel to the Arctic Circle. In its southern reaches, the forest includes a number of deciduous species, birch among them, and grows to a density of some 130 tons per acre. In the north, one finds at most a density of 45 tons per acre, principally larch. Given its average productivity of roughly 7 tons per acre per year, the taiga could supply the entire earth with wood from now until the end of time, but unfortunately—or fortunately—most of it is inaccessible.

The taiga is characterized by conifers (spruce, fir, Scotch pine, and Siberian stone pine, among others), which are excellently adapted to the cold. Their "leaves" are reduced to needles, which limits their surface area and the plants' water loss. In addition, the stomata, the microscopic pores that allow gas exchange in summer, are totally closed in winter, transforming the tree into a sort of hibernating mummy. Larches behave like deciduous trees and shed their "breathing organs" in winter. Losing little water in summer through their needles and none at all in winter, larches combine the advantages of the deciduous tree and the conifer, which helps explain their remarkable success in the taiga.

Be there a will, and

wisdom finds a way.

George Crabbe

If the horse's load is poorly balanced or improperly tied, it will not last the day, especially in steep mountains.

Fire

Nothing is more important on an expedition than the fire. Camp life revolves around it. Whether built to last an hour or a week, the fire is always at the center of everything. The Tofalar people, with whom we traveled on horseback in Siberia, say that a fire is born when it is lit, lives while it burns, and dies when it is put out—such is the material and symbolic importance of fire to this forest people.

Making a Fire in Summer

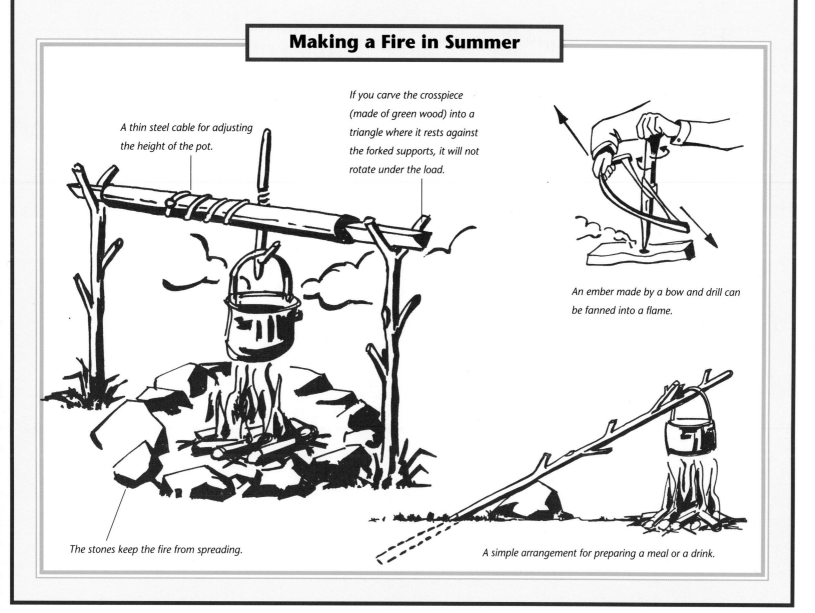

A thin steel cable for adjusting the height of the pot.

If you carve the crosspiece (made of green wood) into a triangle where it rests against the forked supports, it will not rotate under the load.

An ember made by a bow and drill can be fanned into a flame.

The stones keep the fire from spreading.

A simple arrangement for preparing a meal or a drink.

I have already explained how to build a fire without matches or a lighter. Master this skill before jumping off into the wilderness and you'll never be without your fire-making implements. Fire is the essential requirement for survival, especially in winter, of course. Then there is the question of food. Here are a few hints.

Snares for Spruce Grouse, Hare, and Other Game

It's easy to catch large spruce grouse. Make a noose out of brass wire and attach it to the end of a pole, as shown in the drawing below. The trick is to move very slowly. With a little practice you can catch one 50 percent of the time—enough to sustain you.

But the porcupine, a fat rodent weighing 15 to 18 pounds, is far and away the most important animal for survival—in fact, backwoodsmen avoid killing it for this very reason. Porcupines are easy to catch since they don't run away but instead just roll up into a spiny ball or threaten with their quilled tails—watch out, they have a range of about six feet! But a good knock with a stick will do the job. And porcupine meat can be eaten raw.

Above: In the north, animals are so unused to traps that there is hardly any need to camouflage them.

Above: Stockade trap. When a lynx grabs the bait, the closing mechanism is triggered.

Left: A snare for hare, with a sprung bough to lift the game out of reach of nonhuman predators.

In country where rabbits are plentiful, you can catch them by putting snares along a run. In winter, the runs are easy to find. In the summer, it can be more complicated, but a good place to look for rabbit trails is in the dense growth of alders and willows by a stream.

On summer nights, fish can be caught without a hook by building a fire on the bank of a lake or river. Fish tend to follow the shoreline and are attracted by the light. Tie a noose on the end of a pole, pass the loop very gently over the fish until it is behind the first set of fins, and then give a slight jerk to tighten it. During their annual run, salmon are so easy to catch in places that you don't even need a snare. Just bend down and scoop them up.

Eating duck, goose, and gull eggs is a good way to fend off starvation in spring and summer. All are edible.

Edible Plants

It is useful to be acquainted with edible plants, even when survival is not at stake. Here is a little list:

- **Canada dogwood:** Scarlet fruit. The Indians used it to make pudding.
- **Labrador tea:** Found especially in bogs.
- **Sap of the quaking aspen:** It is collected in spring by scoring an aspen's trunk after removing the bark and is then dried in the sun. The sap, which keeps well, was used by the Indians to make flour for a kind of bread. The taste is quite sweet and not unpleasant.
- **Black crowberry:** In Siberia, the juice of the crowberry is mixed with water. The Even people add it to fish and reindeer meat as a condiment.
- **Lichen:** When the larder is empty it can be boiled in soup or made into bread.
- **Wild rhubarb:** It is edible raw or can be boiled into a compote. It is excellent and chock full of vitamins.
- **Root of the frog lily:** Rich in starch, this plant is highly edible.

These are just some of the many edible plants found in the northlands, and I haven't even included berries (the strawberry and blueberry among them) and mushrooms (which require much caution, though practically all that grow in the north are edible). It's best to pack a small book that has a complete list of the edible plants, berries, and mushrooms, illustrated with drawings or photos, and try to find them along the way.

Another kind of sprung bough.

Vitus Bering

In 1725, Russian Czar Peter the Great, struggling to turn his country toward the West, chose Danish explorer Vitus Bering to explore what lay beyond Siberia. It took three years for one of Bering's expeditions to arrive on the west coast of the Kamchatka Peninsula, a distance of 13,000 miles. Bering set sail on July 13, 1728, discovered St. Lawrence Island, then headed through the strait separating Asia from America. Another expedition was subsequently undertaken. This enterprise was colossal in scale, with multiple goals (most of them geopolitical), and nine hundred members—scientists, sailors, and servants. Thousands of tons of equipment, as well as all the material they would need to build their ships, had to be brought by horse and boat across Siberia. It took eight years!

Once the ships were ready, surmounting huge odds, the navigators finally sailed eastward, and on July 16, 1741, Bering sighted the St. Elias mountains on the other side of the strait. He had reached his goal: *Al-ey-as-ka*, meaning literally "the land beyond the seas."

Racked with scurvy, however, he simply shrugged his shoulders at seeing the long-sought land and turned back. The return trip was a doleful one. The ship rounded the Aleutians and came to grief in November on the rocky shores of an island where the expedition settled to wait out a horrible winter. Many of the men died there, including Bering himself, for whom the island was later named. Years later, Captain James Cook christened the passage separating Asia and America the Bering Strait.

Travel on horseback can either be a great pleasure (right), or a total nightmare, as in the following photograph, of crossing a rock-strewn slope, where every step is a hard-won victory.

Lake Baikal in a Fishing Boat

AFTER TRAVELING for four months in the unearthly mountains of northern Mongolia, we arrived one evening at a pass from which we looked down on the oldest lake in the world stretched out below us. Startled and moved, we remembered what the Siberians had been telling us all along: "It's not a lake. It's a sea."

We would have ample opportunity to discover this firsthand on our lengthwise crossing of the lake, covering a distance of more than five hundred miles, rowing the whole way. Because of our small boat, which we bought in a fishing village, and the winds that can rise suddenly to gale force, we were forced to make many detours and follow the shoreline closely. It would take us two months to work our way up the lake, a concept that startled more than one fisherman. Why spend so much time when a motorboat could do the trip in two days?

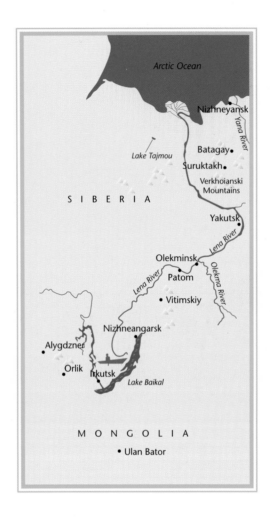

We were in no hurry. We could watch the silvery fish pass under our boat to a depth of a hundred feet. Once, on rounding a rock, we saw a bear. And seals raised their heads out of the water to stare at us with large round eyes. We enjoyed seeing the shoreline unfold, with its vistas of beaches, mountains, forests, and green prairies. After a week on the water we were delighted to arrive at a small village of omul (a fish native to Lake Baikal) fishermen.

Silent and natural, rowing awakens the senses and puts you in harmony with the landscape. Above all, it made us open and attentive to the slightest movement of the animals and humans, too, who are the soul of a wild country.

As agents of our own movement, we felt the water, the wind, the swell. The landscape enveloped us. We were one with the lake.

Most of the ports are on the southern end of the lake, which has readier access to Irkutsk, the capital of Siberia, through which the Lake Baikal catch is routed.

Preserving and Preparing Fish and Meat

In hot summer weather, there is only one good way to keep blowflies from laying their eggs on meat or fish, and that is to submerge it in brine. Many Indians and other local people smoke their meat, but the larvae burrow into it nonetheless. Smoking fish is easier, and in any case it improves the taste. Here is how it is done: Choose small trout, ten to fourteen inches long, and gut them without removing the heads. Soak them in brine for twenty-four hours. Hang them by the tail from sticks hung across the top of a smokehouse, which can be made of stone, canvas, bark, or even a metal drum from which both ends have been removed (this works very well). The smoke is provided by a fire that is not too hot, in which bits of firewood are mixed with rotten ash or birch. The fish is ready after forty-eight hours and will keep for about a month.

In winter, there is no problem keeping food or protecting it from flies—living in a freezer has its advantages. The only hitch is that when temperatures drop very low (below –40° F), thawing meat and fish is a problem. No one wants to stand around the stove for two hours while dinner thaws, especially after a long day of tramping in the cold. The easiest method is to submerge the food in water, either directly when a river is open or by cutting a hole through the ice, and leave it there while you make camp. The meat or fish will be thawed a half-hour later, much more rapidly than over a fire.

Lake Baikal

This freshwater sea forms a giant crescent almost four hundred miles long but only fifty miles across at its widest point. This lake holds all the records. It is the largest freshwater lake in Eurasia and the deepest in the world (5,715 feet). It represents the world's greatest liquid freshwater resource and has the purest water! It contains as much fresh water as the Great Lakes, 20 percent of the world's reserves! Three hundred and thirty-six rivers flow into it, but only one—the Angara—flows out. Lake Baikal is host to twenty-six hundred species of plants and animals, three-quarters of which are found nowhere else in the world. The best-known example is Baikal's freshwater seal, of which there are 300,000.

But not all is idyllic in this natural wonder, ringed by high mountains whose glaciers sit at more than 10,000 feet. For one thing, there are the renowned paper-processing plants, each spilling up to ten million cubic feet of polluted water per day into the southern part of the lake, and polluting the air with their sulfur dioxide emissions. Then there are the many plans under development to enhance the local tourist industry: hotel chains, amusement parks, sports centers, and ski resorts. And the valuable omul is being overfished, which threatens to disrupt the lake's ecosystem.

As usual, humans are putting pressure on the goose that lays the golden eggs. Will classifying the lake as one of the great natural areas of the world preserve what some call the Sea of Baikal?

We "galley slaves" changed places promptly every twenty minutes.

The Siberian Musk-Deer, or Kabarga

When we arrived in Siberia we had never even heard of this animal. Imagine our surprise when, on our second night out, Kika, one of our Tofalar guides, moved off a short distance from camp, blew eight or ten times into his birch-bark whistle, fired a shot, and returned in ten minutes with a kabarga!

Find an area rich in deer before using the whistle.

The kabarga is a small deer of twenty pounds or so that is found in all of southern Siberia, mainly in wooded and mountainous areas. Tofalar hunters kill a great many for their meat, but also for their musk, which they sell to the Japanese, who use it as a perfume base. The hunter attracts the deer by blowing into a whistle carved out of birch bark that imitates the distress call of the kabarga fawn. Both bucks and does run up to investigate, sometimes coming from considerable distances. They stop just a few yards from the hunter, who has only a brief opportunity to shoulder his gun and fire, since kabarga are very quick. The meat is rich and well flavored. In summer, the kabarga was our main fare. It was the perfect warm-weather game since we could polish one off quickly and didn't need to store any leftovers.

Two of the kabarga's distinctive traits: the hyperdeveloped canine and the musk sac.

Crossing Central Siberia with Thirty Sled Dogs

"YOU'RE CRAZY!" With some variations, this was the unanimous response of Siberians to the news that we would try a dogsled crossing of the mountains between Lake Baikal and the Lena River in the dead of winter. And the Siberian winter is no myth. For three months of the year, while we would be traveling with our thirty dogs, the temperature dips constantly into the extreme range. The hardest thing at –60° F is getting through the night. It is impossible to sleep for more than an hour at a time, because your breath freezes and the frost cakes up and blocks the small opening through which you breathe, swaddled in your sleeping bag.

It's impossible to heat the tent. It would take hours of work in the evening to collect a sufficient supply of firewood, and someone would have to stay awake watching it to make sure the tent didn't go up in flames. This is

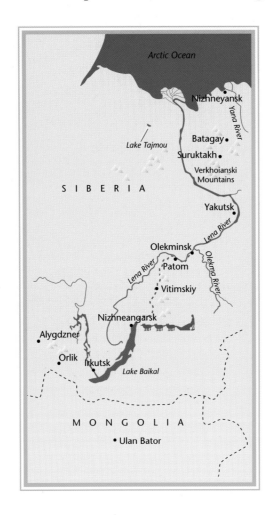

the great paradox when you're dealing with extreme cold: You are always either too warm or too cold. There is no middle ground.

After the freezing nights came the days and weeks of exhausting walking through a country where the sun had stopped shining. To make matters worse, our team was no longer functioning as a unit and had long since stopped trying. Each member retreated into himself, a cure worse than the illness. Soon the days brought nothing but suffering, and the cold was the least of it.

Only the wolves howling under the varied and astonishing displays of the aurora borealis and the grandeur of a country still untouched by human aggression gave us any reason to go on, to continue plodding northward, advancing also toward the spring that would bring back light and sunshine to the earth, which, despite its pettiness, is enduringly fascinating.

In –75° F weather, we made camp with care and made sure to have a good supply of firewood on hand. Finding a standing dead tree became an important priority toward nightfall. But we let the fire go out in the tent at night, and we slept fully dressed, still wearing our sheepskins, dozing fitfully and waiting for morning to come.

Dead trees that are dry and still standing make the warmest fire.

It is astonishing how many people die in the mountains or in the north surrounded by one of the best insulators—snow. Find a slope or a hillside where exposure to the wind has packed the snow well and dig out a burrow. Just as in an igloo, the temperature inside can quickly rise to around 32° F, even in –50° F weather, particularly if you have a candle. With a bit more time and some wood you can make yourself quite a good shelter. It takes only a few branches, although a tarp helps. Site the shelter at the foot of a rise and dig down to the ground. That way, a current of warm air will carry the smoke up along the slope and reflect the heat better into the hole.

Although the extremities feel the cold first, it does no good after a point to add more layers of gloves when your hands are cold. It's the rest of the body that needs to be kept warm.

A Siberian trapper taught us how to make these boots, the warmest we ever found. They are sewn together from squares of half-inch-thick felt and work beautifully even in the bitterest weather.

Knowing Where North Is

Popular wisdom to the contrary, the one sure way to find the north is to use a compass. The sky is often not clear enough to locate the sun or stars accurately.

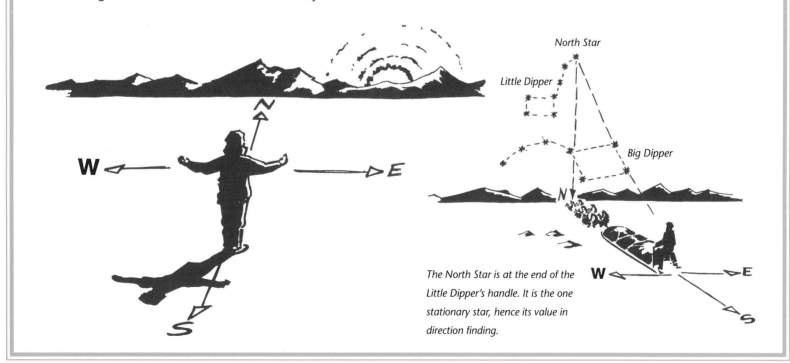

The North Star is at the end of the Little Dipper's handle. It is the one stationary star, hence its value in direction finding.

Resting the dogs for even a half-hour during the middle of the day can do them tremendous good, especially if you can stop when the sun is shining, a rare luxury.

Dogsleds

A heavy shock cord reduces the impact on the dogs of the sled hitting an obstacle.

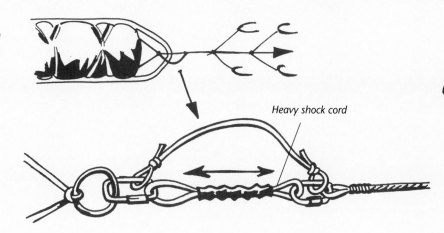

Heavy shock cord

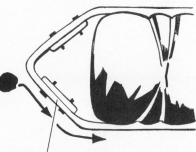

Bumpers are pointed to push obstructions aside.

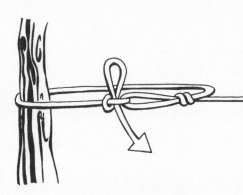

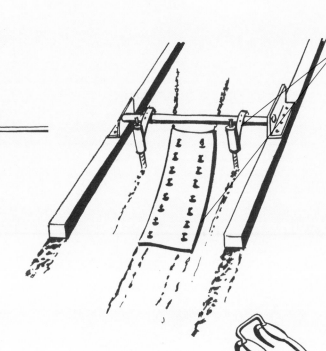

The sleds have two types of brakes: a plate for deep snow, and threaded rods for ice. The rods are screwed deeper into the mounts as they wear away.

A Musher's Glossary

- A *musher* is a dogsled driver. The term comes from the old startup command "Mush!" derived from the French word *marche* (go).
- The *lead dog* runs at the head of the team and interprets the musher's voice commands.
- The *swing dogs* are the pair immediately behind the lead dog. They help bring the team around whenever a change in direction is called for.
- The *wheel dogs* are the pair immediately in front of the sled. They are generally very powerful animals.
- The *team dogs* are the rank-and-file members of the dog team.

The snow anchor keeps the dogs from starting without the musher.

The basic harness. While other kinds exist, this one is widely used.

Building an Igloo

"The igloo is at once a masterful design and the evanescent symbol of a world where all is temporary, all is in movement."

Top of the igloo; last block

The first three blocks

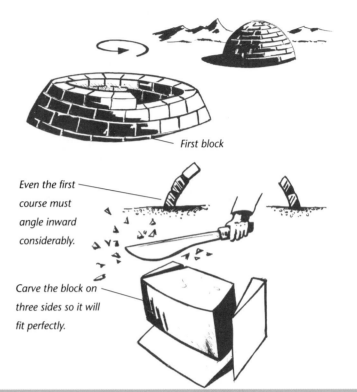

First block

Even the first course must angle inward considerably.

Carve the block on three sides so it will fit perfectly.

Dig the rectangular blocks from a trench in wind-packed snow.

We were the first Europeans to enter the village of Patom, lost in the mountains of Yakutia. And we welcomed the prospect of spending a few days there to recover, having just traveled nonstop for two months through the bitter Siberian cold.

Frozen Lakes and Rivers

While lakes and rivers are the only really useful highways through the wilderness in winter, you quickly learn that ice can be either your best ally or your worst enemy. Overflow—when the water rises onto the ice surface—and slush—when the overflow mixes with snow—are conditions that can slow a sled team drastically or even bring it to a halt. The worst, though, is when the snow hides a layer of ice that is too thin to hold the weight of a person, let alone a sled.

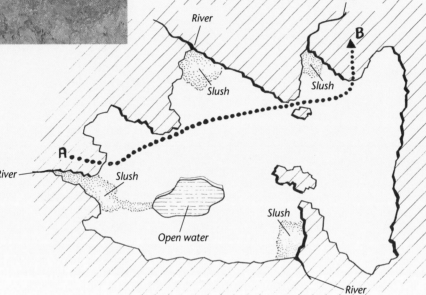

Slush may form almost anywhere on a lake, but by retracing your steps the moment you encounter it, you can generally find a way to go around it. Avoid river and stream inlets, where slush is almost always found.

Slush and Overflow

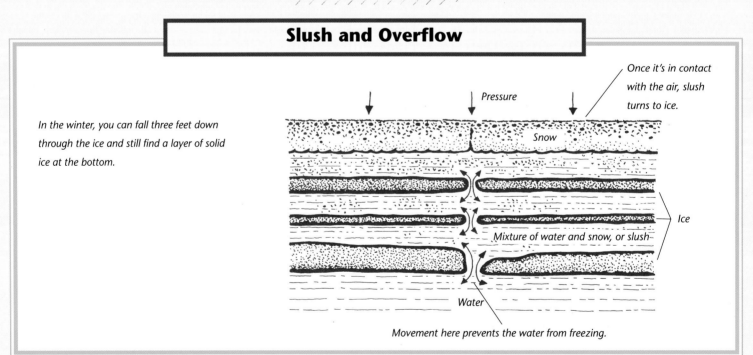

In the winter, you can fall three feet down through the ice and still find a layer of solid ice at the bottom.

172

Through Yakutia by Pony Sled on Frozen River Roads

THE MAIN DIFFERENCE between the pony and the sled dog is that the dog is very eager to pull and to travel, and the pony would prefer to stay in the barn. Yet the Yakut pony is the ideal means of transportation in this region, since it's very well adapted to the extreme cold and is skilled at traveling on frozen rivers. Besides, everyone in the area uses ponies, so when we passed through a village, no one stared at us. We had the same sled, same ponies, same clothes, same fur caps as they did—and even our faces, weathered from travel, had the look of the country. This is what we had wanted—to cross Siberia and become part of its landscape, respecting its traditions. But the Siberians we met found this disappointing. They had never seen foreigners before, and our appearance did not live up to expectations. It's as though a Martian were to appear at a Paris café, climb out of a Peugeot with a baguette under his arm, and announce, "Hi, I'm a Martian!"

No, what they wanted were real

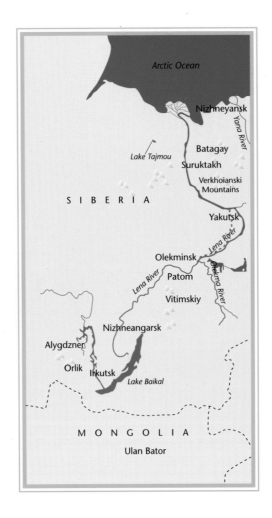

Frenchmen, and to prove that we were real we had to produce our passports, speak French, and Volodya (our Russian interpreter) had to spit on the ground and swear it was the truth. Only then could the party begin.

The news would spread like wildfire, and those who lived outside the village were called in. The best food the villagers had to offer was presented, and all available vodka was requisitioned. We had to tell our stories and talk about France and the French—and on no account could we dwell on our expedition or our ponies. These subjects couldn't have mattered less to the Siberians, since they spend their lives on their ponies' backs. We had to describe Paris, the clothes Parisians wear, what they do, what they say. In return, the Siberians offered us all they knew and had. Their generosity was complete and unstinting.

The next day we would resume our long glide along the frozen river, assuming there was no blizzard, no piled-up ice, and no deep snow to slow us down.

Winter lasts twelve months in Siberia.

The rest of the year is summer.

Siberian saying

We traveled along the frozen Lena River as far as Yakutsk. Every year the Siberians make a road on the Lena that is used to transport supplies to the farms and villages strung out at pony distance (thirty to forty miles) along the river. It is one of the rare six-hundred-mile roads to have the luxury of being resurfaced annually.

Carl, a pony breeder, never imagined that he would leave his collective farm to travel with a group of Frenchmen, yet perestroika made it possible for him to do just that. He stayed with us for two months. We'll never forget the long stories he told about his country, nor the distinctive tenor our expedition took on because of him and his extroverted good humor.

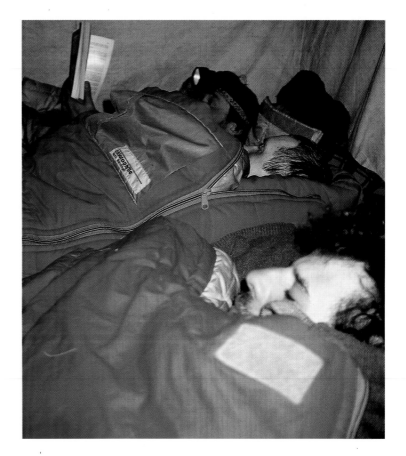

You always bring a few books on an expedition, but the rare moments of peace tend to be for catching up on sleep.

Yakut ponies can travel in –60° F weather with no difficulty, since they are both genetically adapted and physically conditioned to extreme conditions. They are able to carry a load of two hundred to three hundred pounds thirty to forty miles a day. This is a cardinal fact in local human society, as the villages are spaced exactly this distance apart. The driver sits on the sled and guides it using two big leather straps that act as reins. By pulling back on them, he can make the ponies walk backward.

The Sled and Harness

The Yakut all use this simple and efficient type of harness, which, like the sled, is made of wood and leather.

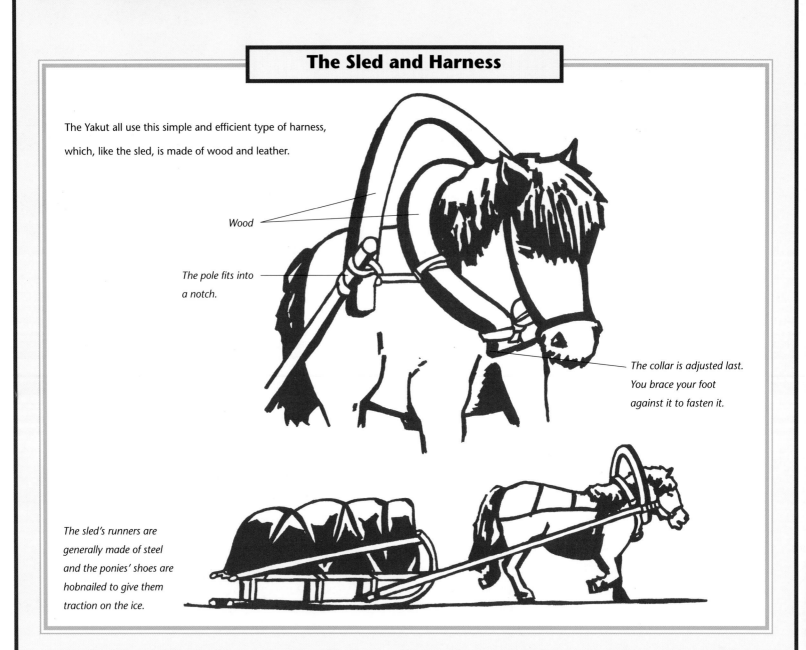

Wood

The pole fits into a notch.

The collar is adjusted last. You brace your foot against it to fasten it.

The sled's runners are generally made of steel and the ponies' shoes are hobnailed to give them traction on the ice.

Knots

When on expedition, it is essential to tie knots that will hold. "The right knot at the right time" would make a good motto for an expedition.

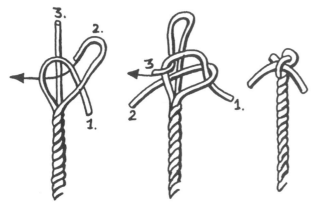

To stop a three-strand rope or cable from unraveling

A strong and efficient knot for tying a line to a post or tree.

Siberian children are used to the cold, but schools close when the temperature drops to –60° F, both to safeguard the children's health and to save on heating bills.

Except for the few Siberians who live in cities, the inhabitants of the region for the most part work the land or, more rarely, live by fishing and trapping.

Crossing the Verkhoianski Mountains with the Nomadic Even

OUR ENCOUNTER with the Even, a nomadic people of the Siberian Arctic who travel through the mountains with their families and herds of reindeer, was unquestionably one of the highlights of this expedition. We found ourselves in contact with a people living in harmony with nature, maintaining a most perfect and beautiful equilibrium.

The Even are not ashamed to travel in the old way in an era of helicopters and snowmobiles. They are not ashamed to set off for the highest peaks to hunt mountain sheep, their main autumn food, in an era when meat is displayed in rows on refrigerated supermarket shelves. They are not ashamed, in an era of television and video games, to remain true to the old ways that the elders pass along to the young during long winter evenings in a tent. On the contrary. They are aware of the differences, and they are conscious that their lifestyle is an art. They

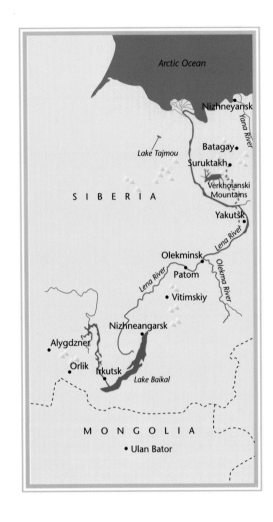

take pride in their mode of existence and pursue it with dignity.

After traveling by dogsled over pack ice that the Inuit cross in snowmobiles, after riding through the Rockies in constant fear of all-terrain vehicles, and after canoeing on arctic rivers invaded by outboard motors, I finally had the feeling among the Even that I had gone back in time. I was no longer following in the footsteps of a vanished people, or walking an abandoned trail time had erased. The Even were here around me, alive and welcoming, an embodiment of the perennial forces that underlie civilization and provide it with depth and richness.

The Even lifestyle meshed with my own ideal image of travel and a life in nature. I spent six wonderful months with these people, and when I left the clan, promising to return, the soul of the Even had in some part taken root in me.

Eva, nine, and Sergei, ageless, were part of the family I lived and traveled with for six months. Nomads and reindeer herders, the Even live in clans composed of several families. They travel with their herds of two to three thousand reindeer, wintering in the valleys and spending the summers on the high plateaus.

Fishing in Winter

There is nothing easier than fishing in summer, but it's a whole different story in winter, when the ice on some Siberian lakes and rivers is six to ten feet thick. You have to dig for two hours before you can even start to fish.

Extending a Net Under the Ice

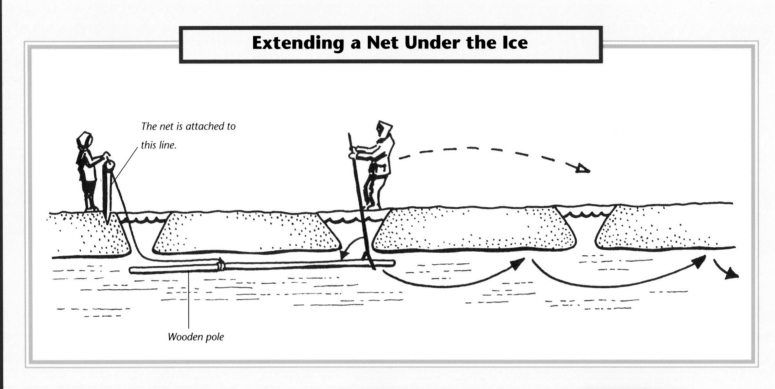

The net is attached to this line.

Wooden pole

Once the pole has been passed from hole to hole under the ice, the net is attached to the line and pulled through. The next day when the net is hauled in, the line is obviously left to run out so that the net can easily be reset. The middle holes are allowed to freeze over, leaving only two holes to be maintained. It's not enough just to dig through the ice. The tricky part is doing so in the right place. Both on lakes and rivers, look for deep spots, trying to locate them based on the surrounding topography. Obviously there is no question of making soundings.

Making a Hole Through the Ice

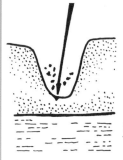

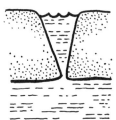

Don't do this, or you'll end up with a hole that is too narrow and the water will prevent you from widening it. Also, it will close up again very quickly.

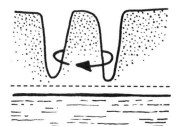

Dig in a circle, so you obtain a plug of ice.

Constantly check that you are digging to the same depth all the way around, or you'll end up with an unusable hole.

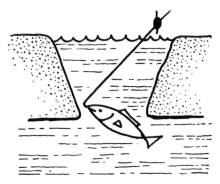

This method produces a hole that is wide enough for fishing.

In Siberia, toward the end of winter, we decided to fish on a lake in the high mountains two hours away by reindeer sled. We were desperately hungry. On reaching the lake, we dug a hole through six feet of ice, a job that took us two more hours, only to find that the lake had frozen solid to the bottom. Digging a new hole took us another two hours! Meanwhile tempers flared and spiteful remarks of the "I told you so" variety flew back and forth.

To Build a Fire

An Even lighting a fire in the shelter of an overturned sled.

When it has been raining for hours and hours, and everything is sopping wet, it's no time to bungle the fire. Your best move is to find a standing dead tree, fell it, and saw it into logs before starting the fire, as described below. In spring, summer, and fall, you must always have, in addition to your tent, a tarpaulin that can be hung near the fire so that you don't get wet faster from the rain than you get dry from being by the fire!

A Wet-Weather Fire

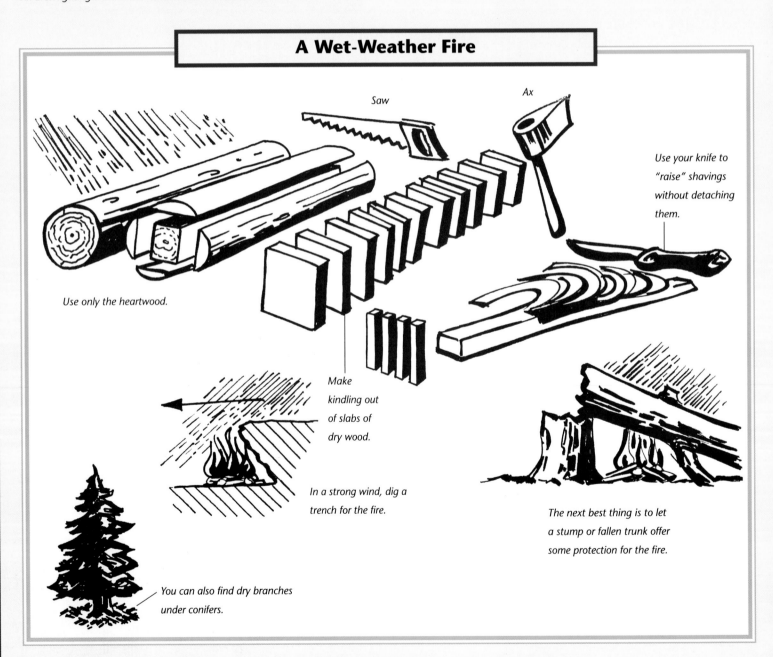

Saw

Ax

Use your knife to "raise" shavings without detaching them.

Use only the heartwood.

Make kindling out of slabs of dry wood.

In a strong wind, dig a trench for the fire.

The next best thing is to let a stump or fallen trunk offer some protection for the fire.

You can also find dry branches under conifers.

The landscape conveys
an impression of absolute
permanence. It is not hostile.
It is simply there—untouched,
silent, and complete.

Edmund Carpenter

Reindeer don't obey voice commands, even after years of training. You have to hold a stick over their heads to direct them—up to the right to make them turn left, and vice versa.

The arctic hare, a very common animal in the Verkhoianski Mountains.

Opposite: Nicolaï was the head of the Even clan that took me in. He was my "Dersu Uzala." Later, he got sick, and, not wanting to become a burden to his clan, he took his own life in 1995. The clan is now led by his brother Vassili.

Although reindeer sleds appear disconcertingly simple, making one requires a real feel for wood and a violin maker's accuracy in determining the size of the different elements.

The harness system, on the other hand, has to be quite ingenious to compensate for the reindeer's limited intelligence.

Reindeer Harness

As many as fifty sleds can be harnessed together in single file, pulled by a hundred reindeer and stretching out over a thousand feet.

Maximum load 110 pounds

Leath

The runners are carved from a slender pine tree that has been soaked in water and bent to the right shape.

The sled is about ten feet long and two and a half feet wide. Dowels are used throughout. The various pieces of wood that go into it—three ax-hewn boards, two wooden runners, and the stanchions, called "dolls" because they look like little figurines—are lashed together with rawhide.

The leader of the clan or one of his sons rides here, at the head of the snaking line of sleds and reindeer, choosing the route.

The reindeer are hitched in pairs.

The Even collect reindeer antlers (in the spring, with the velvet still on) and sell them to the Japanese, who consider antlers to be an excellent aphrodisiac. This provides the Even with the cash to hire a helicopter to transport food and equipment or evacuate a tribe member who is injured or sick. Such a change represents considerable progress for the Even. Will they always use the cash wisely?

Saddling a Reindeer

Unlike a horse's hide, a reindeer's hide floats loose on its back, and its hips sway as it walks, which makes it hard for a rider to stay balanced. At four, an Even child has already spent many hours loaded on the back of a reindeer and can sit in the saddle for several hours.

By the age of six, an Even boy owns two or three reindeer. He rides them in rotation to round up or drive the herd of reindeer under his care.

The Saddle, the Reindeer, and the Rider

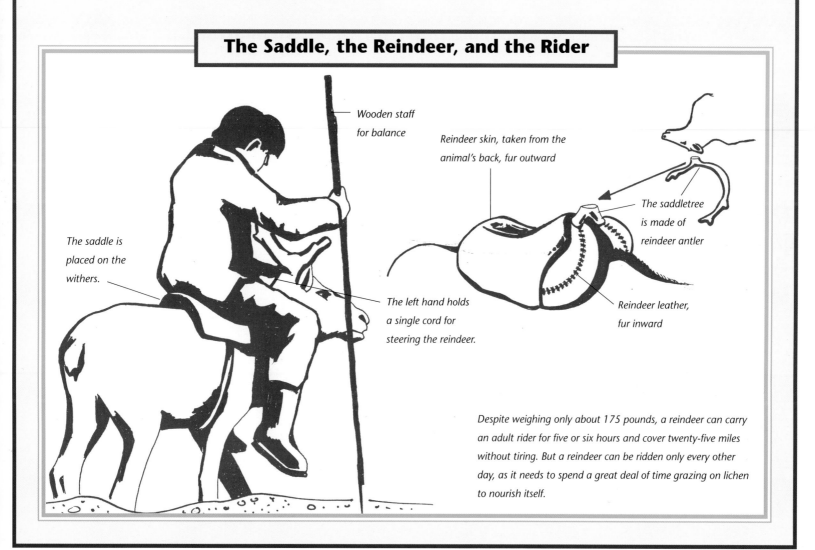

Wooden staff for balance

Reindeer skin, taken from the animal's back, fur outward

The saddletree is made of reindeer antler

The saddle is placed on the withers.

The left hand holds a single cord for steering the reindeer.

Reindeer leather, fur inward

Despite weighing only about 175 pounds, a reindeer can carry an adult rider for five or six hours and cover twenty-five miles without tiring. But a reindeer can be ridden only every other day, as it needs to spend a great deal of time grazing on lichen to nourish itself.

Some Important Knots

Clove hitch

This is a practical knot, for it can be tied very quickly. Its one drawback for use with animals is that it can be difficult to untie if an animal pulls hard on it.

Eskimo bowline

This is the knot. If you could only have one knot, this would be the one to choose. It can be tied in four seconds and loosened in a quarter second.

However hard you pull on it, it won't jam. We use it with dogs, horses, reindeer—pretty much everywhere and with everything. It's the king of knots.

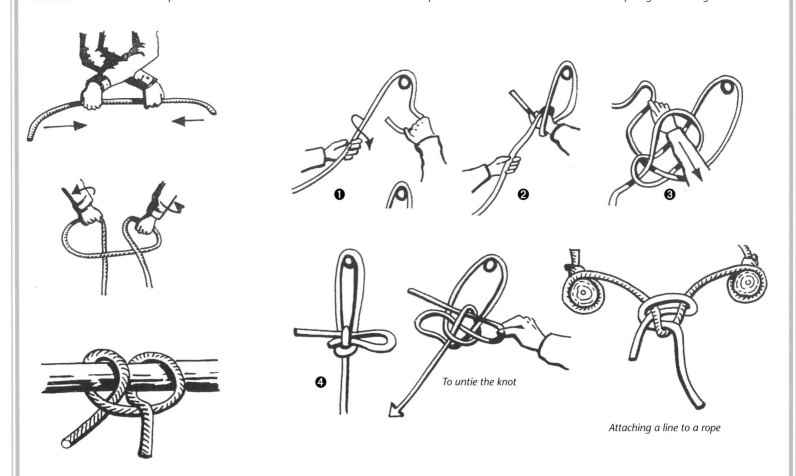

To untie the knot

Attaching a line to a rope

Swaddled in furs and blankets and held in place by boards on either side, babies generally travel at night, when there are fewer mosquitoes. These insects can be very fierce in the heat of an arctic day.

Opposite: Handing out salt, which can be used to keep the reindeer near camp if necessary.

Other than reindeer meat, the Even mainly eat
bread in the form of a flat cake. Their drink is
tea, to the tune of three or four quarts a day per
person. Much more rarely, but with a total lack
of moderation, they drink the holy liquor vodka,
usually after the helicopter has visited.

At the age of seven or eight, girls start working—
helping their mothers with the younger children,
milking the reindeer, and performing a variety of
household tasks, including sewing and cooking.

The staple of the Even diet is reindeer meat, and every part of the animal—innards, bones, and hide—is used.

By the time they're eight years old, Even children have their own lassos of braided reindeer hide and are able to catch a galloping animal at twenty yards.

Whipping

This is a good way to bind the end of a rope to keep it from fraying. Whipping is also used to keep wooden tool handles or stakes from splitting. The skill is fairly easy to master.

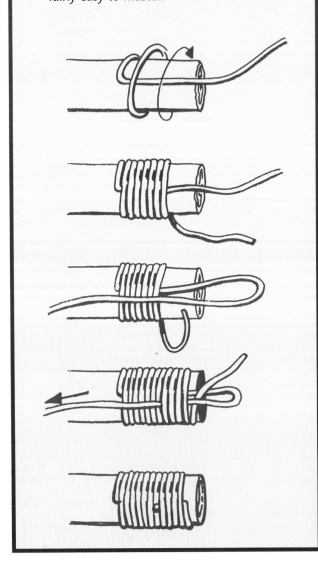

A reindeer's pack load is much the same as a horse's, except that the same saddle is used for packing and riding. The load can be up to about a hundred pounds, divided into two equal parts.

I finally had the

feeling I had gone

back in time.

Siberian Arctic: Descending the Yana River

AFTER WE ENDURED the legendary cold of the Siberian winter, the summer heat almost did us in. The sun shines all day and night on the Yana River, and at midday the mercury can climb over 105° F.

You might think that would be better than a temperature of –75° F, but you would be wrong. At –75° F, there are many things you can do to make yourself warmer. You can add another layer of clothes, build a fire, move around, eat fatty foods—a whole long list. But there is not a thing you can do to protect yourself from the heat, other than dive into the water as the elk do to escape the clouds of mosquitoes, horseflies, and gnats that swarm at the water's surface. At night—or rather during the portion of the day we set aside for sleeping—we took shelter under our mosquito nets, which we had carefully set out in the shade. Our dog Otchum also disliked the heat and would dig himself a burrow to sleep in.

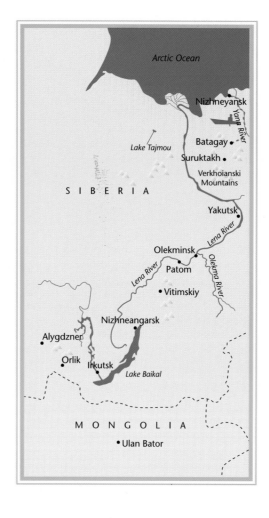

The ground thaws only to a depth of twenty to thirty inches and the permafrost underlying it holds many carcasses from the Ice Age. We unearthed mammoth teeth, a tusk, and various bones.

The Yana River, which would carry our boats down to the Arctic Ocean, loops through the tundra, cutting away at its banks so that whole sections collapse at a time, sometimes uncovering permafrost that has been frozen for thousands of years. We crossed areas so wild we thought we were about to enter a forgotten land where the mammoth still roamed.

Although we were traveling through space, we were also exploring time, an immemorial and mythical time in which history played no part, and to which Nature alone could give us access. Though slight, our access was of great value—as though Nature granted us a rare privilege by allowing us glimpses of the secrets of the earth she so jealously guarded.

The few villages along the Yana subsist by
fishing, trapping sables, and raising reindeer.
The herds graze in the surrounding tundra,
where thousands of mammoth skeletons lie
buried in the ice. Right: A tibia.

Our handsomest trophy, a mammoth tusk more than six feet long. Unfortunately it was too heavy to bring to our final destination, Nizhneyansk, a small port on the Arctic Ocean. When we reached it after an expedition lasting a year and a half, we found a crowd of more than four hundred people gathered to celebrate our arrival.

The Yana's current was too weak and the headwind too strong for us to drift along lazily. When the wind was against us, we rowed eight to fifteen hours a day in order to reach the Arctic Ocean before the cold set in.

Summer is never long enough or
warm enough to erase winter.

In the summer, especially above the Arctic Circle, it is impossible to sleep without mosquito netting.

Volodya Vladimir Glazounov

Volodya Vladimir Glazounov, aged thirty-five, married, two children, a geologist by profession. He was scheduled to join only one of the six stages of our big trip but ended up participating in all of them. For a year and a half we lived together day and night. Without him, our story would have been very different, for three thousand miles from the capital, perestroika was only a word. Volodya served as my interpreter, go-between, and negotiator. It was he who dealt with the local mafia and civil administration to smooth the obstacles that arose in our path. But the expedition allowed him to dream and to travel as he had never done before. He had no regrets. I'll always remember his last words to me: "Thanks to you, I discovered my country." He died in a helicopter crash in 1995.

Lapland and the Kola Peninsula

AFTER FIFTEEN YEARS of traveling to Arctic wastes around the globe, I had come full circle and was back with my first love.

The first time, we were only sixteen years old. Clutching our student discount tickets, we had climbed aboard the train at the Gare du Nord in Paris with our tent, fishing rod, and backpacks, and had stayed on, heading north, until the last stop—Kiruna, Sweden, above the Arctic Circle. Wide-eyed at the vast space in front of us, we set off on foot across the great plateaus of Lapland, where a few reindeer herders still lived. This was the start of a life inspired by the north.

Fifteen years later, driving my own team of sled dogs with Otchum in the lead, I was again traveling with friends on the great plateaus, planning a trip further east this time, to the Kola Peninsula (in the Soviet Union) in the dead of winter. Otchum was returning to his native country, a land he would never have left had our paths not

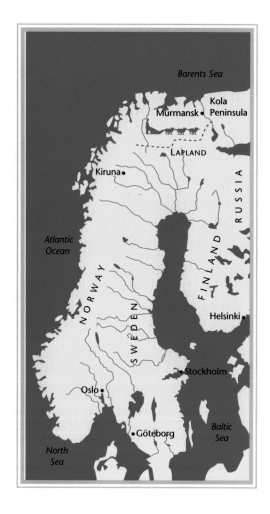

crossed on the shores of Lake Baikal. If I hadn't come along, he would have become a hunting dog.

Jérôme Allouc, who had reared my dog team, was taking part in his first important expedition to the Far North. Later he would travel to northern Quebec to train my dogs and accompany me to the Yukon and Alaska, where I wanted to enter my dog team in the hardest race of all, the Yukon Quest, which runs a thousand miles from Whitehorse to Fairbanks. Pierre Michaux, a member of our Alaska expedition, was returning to the Far North, which he had known only in the summertime.

Our crew was good, and so were our dogs. We made excellent progress through Finland and on the Kola Peninsula, traveling fifty miles a day on beautiful hard trails, packed down by the snowmobiles of reindeer herders. It made excellent training for the full year's expedition for which I was then preparing.

In the spring, when the effects of sun and freezing temperatures combine to create snow that is typically crusty, snowshoes make it possible to walk fairly easily on its surface.

Opposite: Pierre Michaux. A pharmacist and businessman in his spare time, my uncle Pierre loves adventure. After no more than a phone call, he will pack his bags for a three-month expedition to Lapland, Alaska, or the Carpathian Mountains.

*The Northern Lights unfurl their luminous
tendrils across the arctic sky. Auroras are caused
by the solar wind interacting with the earth's
magnetic field. Energetic electrons penetrate the
upper atmosphere and ionize its atoms and
molecules on their course towards the earth's
magnetic poles. The resultant luminosity comes
in a range of colors, the most common being
white, yellow, and green. More rarely, the aurora
may be red, pink, or purple.*

Making Snowshoes

In the old days a backwoodsman could tell who had passed along a trail simply by looking at the snowshoe tracks. Their signature was unmistakable. Snowshoes are rarely used these days and are even more rarely made in the traditional way with wood and leather.

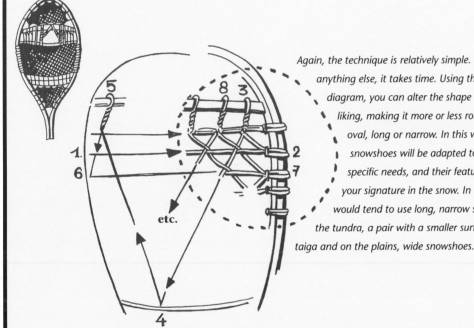

Again, the technique is relatively simple. More than anything else, it takes time. Using the basic diagram, you can alter the shape to your liking, making it more or less round or oval, long or narrow. In this way your snowshoes will be adapted to your specific needs, and their features will be your signature in the snow. In the forest, you would tend to use long, narrow snowshoes; in the tundra, a pair with a smaller surface area; in the taiga and on the plains, wide snowshoes.

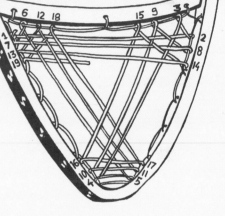

Animals Also Have Snowshoes

The willow ptarmigan in spring.

It has been calculated that the pressure of an animal's paw on snow should not exceed 40 grams per cm^2 for ease of walking. A few examples: the ptarmigan, with its feathered toes, exerts a pressure of 10 grams/cm^2; the snowshoe hare, 19 grams/cm^2; the fox and the lynx, with hair growing between their pads, 20 grams/cm^2. The large spruce grouse, on the other hand, at 50 grams/cm^2, has more trouble walking over the snow, as do deer and boar with pressures of over 300 grams/cm^2. An eminent Russian biologist, Formozov, divides the animals that have to travel on snow into three categories: the chionophobes, for whom fresh-fallen powder is an enemy; the chionophiles, who are actually helped by it; and the chionophores, for whom it is neutral.

While the staple food in summer is fish, in winter it is generally game. One needs large animals such as caribou and moose to feed the dogs and small ones such as partridge, hare, or grouse for the people. Of course, knowing how to find the game is very important, as is mastering the arts of tracking, stalking, and hunting in general.

In winter, you hunt on snowshoes. Preserving the meat afterwards is no problem since the temperature never rises above 0° F.

Preparing Game

Bleed the animal by hanging it head down. The blood, which is rich in vitamins, minerals, and salt, shouldn't go to waste. Skinning comes next, which provides you with the hide or fur and makes it easier to cut up the meat. Then gut the animal, reserving the offal, and cut the meat into usable pieces, keeping some for later, particularly in the winter, when everything is frozen solid.

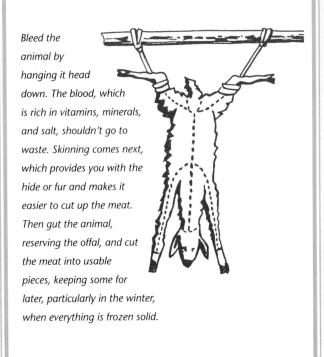

If you hold the knife with the blade facing out, the knife will slide over the intestinal cavity without rupturing it.

On occasion, we have stopped for an entire day to follow spruce grouse on our snowshoes. These birds were our staple food in the Soviet portion of Lapland (Kola Peninsula).

After several weeks traveling eastward through Finland, we again found ourselves among the smiling Russians, a people of rare and spontaneous generosity.

Below: Otchum, back in his native country, with his mate and seven of his sons—Nanook, Baikal, Torok, Voulk, Amarok, Oumiak, and Oukiok— behind him.

On Horseback Toward Lake Thukada

BABY BOTTLE, powdered milk, diapers. These made for a very strange load, at least compared to what I was used to seeing on a packhorse. Everything was designed with *her* in mind: the two-seater saddle, a hot-water bottle for the winter, our daily rhythm, the horses chosen for their docility . . .

Montaine, our little daughter.

Montaine. She is our little queen, who entered the forest at the age of eighteen months and emerged a year later, talking. About what? Bears, wolves, the northern lights, ice, sled dogs. She spent a year looking with absorption at a picture book, the full-scale book of nature. And every day, with her help, we added a new chapter.

We jumped from page to page on horseback through British Columbia toward a big lake I call "Thukada," where Diane, Montaine, and I would prepare for winter by building the cabin of our dreams. When the cold came and froze the country hard

around us, we could then set off with our dogs over the frozen trails.

In the meantime, we had our horses to deal with, four of them, which we had carefully picked from among a thousand others in the nearest city. We wanted them to be experienced, older rather than younger, and above all extremely gentle. Diane rode with Montaine on a saddle that was especially designed for her, but the tired child most often slept, gently rocking, on her mother's back.

Otchum, our old friend, was given the important task of warning us of danger, and the danger we feared most was grizzly bears. You mustn't go too near their young or their fresh kills, and above all you must avoid surprising them. Grizzlies don't wake up in a good mood. Otchum ended up becoming Montaine's tireless playmate. In fact he spent most of his time with the girl, watching over her with a rare and very moving affection.

When you are traveling with horses, it is not always easy to find a good campsite. A number of important elements have to come together: wood, water, grass, and ground flat enough to pitch the tent on. If you can have a spectacular view of the mountains at the same time, you're in heaven.

Opposite: Canada geese are found just about everywhere in Canada. They arrive in springtime at the time of the first thaw and leave at the end of autumn.

I so wanted to see the caribou swim

and the fish in the lake.

That joy, it was my one desire.

Thoughts fell away.

A line that has unspooled.

Inuit song

Crossing rivers was one of the most unpleasant aspects of our journey in British Columbia. Rainfall had been at record levels, and the water was very high, often forcing us to make long detours to find fords, which almost always turned out to be much deeper than expected!

Variously called "the king of the West" and, more prosaically, "the giant deer of the Rockies," the elk, or wapiti, can weigh more than a thousand pounds. Elk antlers are greatly prized by hunters. In fact, between the hunters pursuing their racks and two upper canines on the one hand, and the ones who wanted its meat on the other, the species was very nearly exterminated. Years of protection have enabled it to make a comeback, and elk now thrive in Canada. They have come back to such an extent that 10 percent of the herds can be harvested annually without affecting the population.

What is man without the beasts?
If all the beasts were gone,
man would die from a
great loneliness of spirit.
For whatever happens to the beasts,
soon happens to man.
All things are connected.

From an 1854 letter from Chief Seattle to President Franklin Pierce

When we traveled by horseback, we forced ourselves to find a place to stop for an hour so that Montaine could get some real sleep. Otchum always took it on himself to watch over her.

Life in the bush is not always idyllic. Fatigue, mosquitoes, bad weather, and a host of other circumstances can conspire to wear you down. Diane was always a model of courage, willpower, and perseverance, even if she often suffered inside, particularly from the solitude.

Naptime was sacred. After giving her a bottle,
Diane sang Montaine a song to put her to sleep
while I took care of the horses and prepared a
simple meal. We hit the trail an hour later one
day and soon came across a female mule deer.

Montaine had brought only one book along, but nature provided plenty of other things to look at. Today, there would be a grizzly bear.

Reading Animal Tracks

You can scan the ground for animal sign in both summer and winter to gain information about the environment, where you play the part of predator in your own right. In winter, tracks can be read on the snow as easily as words are in a book, but in summer they are fewer and much harder to find.

The black bear is very common in the forested areas of the Canadian Far North. Its meat is tender and well flavored. It particularly enjoys eating blueberries. Curious by nature, it sometimes approaches quite close to camp.

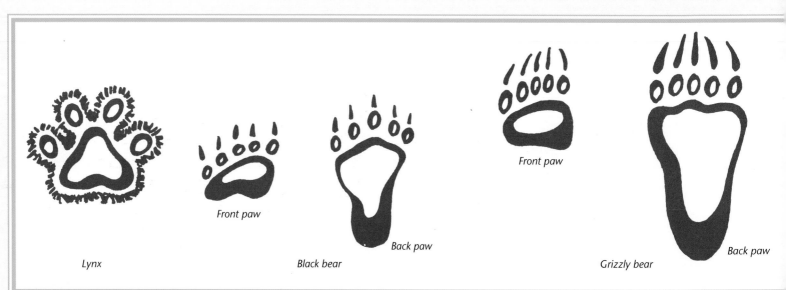

Lynx

Front paw

Back paw

Black bear

Front paw

Back paw

Grizzly bear

Top: The footprint of a ptarmigan and the mark a grouse's wing made at the moment it took flight. Above: The front paw print of a black bear and a rabbit's track.

Wolf

Dog

Porcupine

Our Cabin on a Lake in Canada

A RUSH OF EMOTION overtook us when we suddenly emerged from the forest and found ourselves looking out over the large lake on whose surface were mirrored the snow-covered peaks of the surrounding mountains. I had scouted out this lake ten years before and, overcome by its beauty, promised myself that I would return someday to build a cabin nearby. What child has not dreamt of doing so—building a log cabin in a place like this, so secluded that the nearest house is more than 125 miles away and your only neighbors are bears, wolves, moose, and caribou? The large lake (some 7,500 acres in extent) opens onto a vast landscape. We set the first four pine logs for our cabin only a few yards from the water's edge, with the forest at our backs, on a slight promontory that offered flat ground. A little farther along to our left, the lake emptied into a beautiful river whose joyous murmur tickled our ears as our eyes sought out tall, straight trees in the surrounding forest.

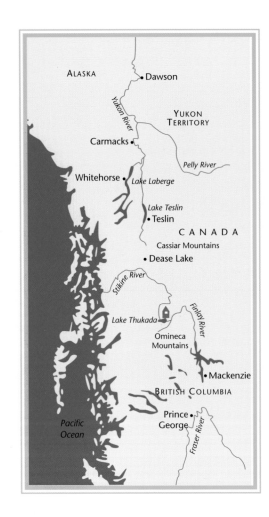

This was the start of six weeks of twelve- to fifteen-hour workdays—felling the trees, removing their bark, hauling them back to the cabin site with the horses, trimming them to equal lengths, notching them, setting them in position, and caulking the seams with moss. Though the tasks were varied, the work was repetitive.

We kept no clock and no calendar. We lived outside of time, in a world our little daughter was discovering with wondering eyes. And we were with her twenty-four hours a day, which was truly one of the great benefits of this journey. It made us smile happily to hear her laugh ring out as she played by the water with her best friend, Otchum. And it made us smile again when we thought of all the people who had thought we were crazy to take our little girl along on such an adventure. In our cabin beside the big lake bathed in light, so free, so happy, with our dogs, and with the majesty of the mountains all around, we *were* crazy, it's true—crazy with happiness.

Building the Log Cabin of Your Dreams

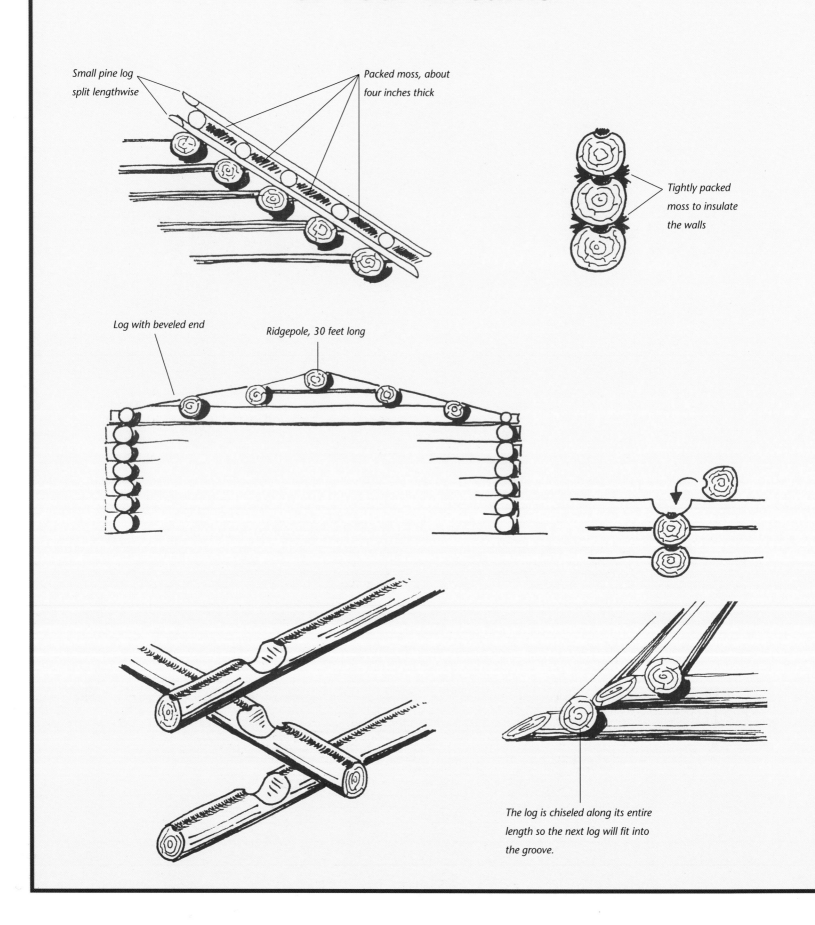

Small pine log split lengthwise

Packed moss, about four inches thick

Tightly packed moss to insulate the walls

Log with beveled end

Ridgepole, 30 feet long

The log is chiseled along its entire length so the next log will fit into the groove.

There is a special tool for chiseling the grooves, but we didn't have one.
We placed the one log above the one to be carved and made markings
from 1 to 5 to indicate the depth of the cut.

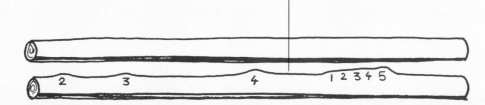

Floor

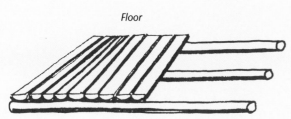

Wooden wedges to make
the floor level

The realized dream

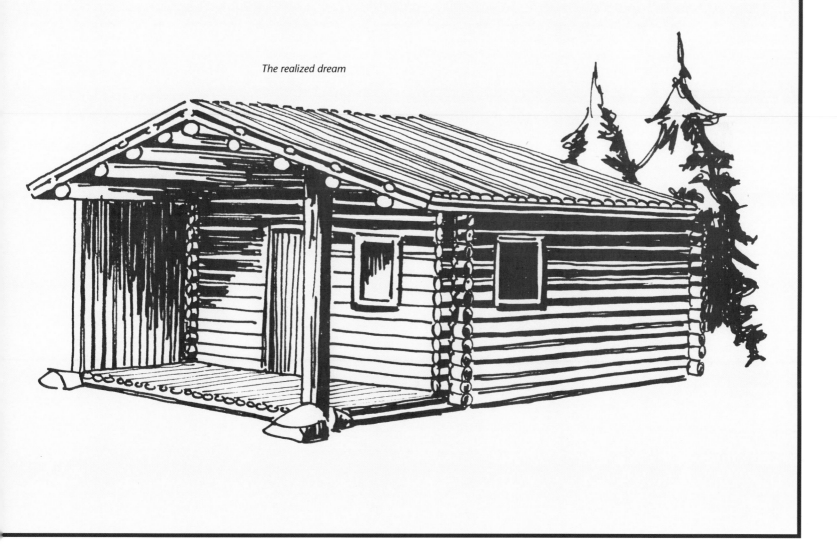

Each day we saw our dream rise a little higher, harmonizing with the landscape, the golden logs set off against the blue of the lake, the green of the forest, and the white of the glaciers.

The hardest part was not actually working on the cabin but deciding where we would build it. The shores of the big lake provided us with many options.

Opposite: We often cut down trees for logs at a considerable distance from our site and brought them in using a horse specially trained for this tricky work.

To make the walls, we used forty-eight logs, each twenty-three feet long and an average of seven inches in diameter. It took about three hours to find, fell, peel, and then haul each log to camp. Setting it in place took another three. In all, you could count on six to eight hours of work per log. Opposite: Luckily, Montaine often lent a hand.

Taking a bath in the most beautiful bathroom in the world. This is a pleasure not to be stinted on, particularly when you are working with pitch-covered pine logs twelve to fifteen hours a day under the hot sun. The water in the lake, which flows directly from the surrounding glaciers, was too cold to swim in.

Since pine is very soft, we made the openings for the door and windows after the walls were completed. For the roof, we first nailed down a layer of half-round logs. We covered this with cross logs and filled the six-inch space between the two layers with moss. Finally we placed a second layer of half-round logs over the whole thing, this time with the cut side outward to shed the rain. Insulated in this way, we were warm in the cabin even when the outdoor temperature was −60° F.

Opposite: Otchum, our lead dog and the dominant male in the pack, makes a small clarification. Voulk is submissive, offering no resistance.

We often had to hunt to feed the dog team. Right: An elk.

Tailor-Made Moccasins

Traditionally used by Indians and frontiersmen, moccasins made of moose or caribou hide are the best footwear for snowshoeing. Your feet breathe and at the same time stay warm. Moccasins also allow your toes to grip by enabling them to feel the ground.

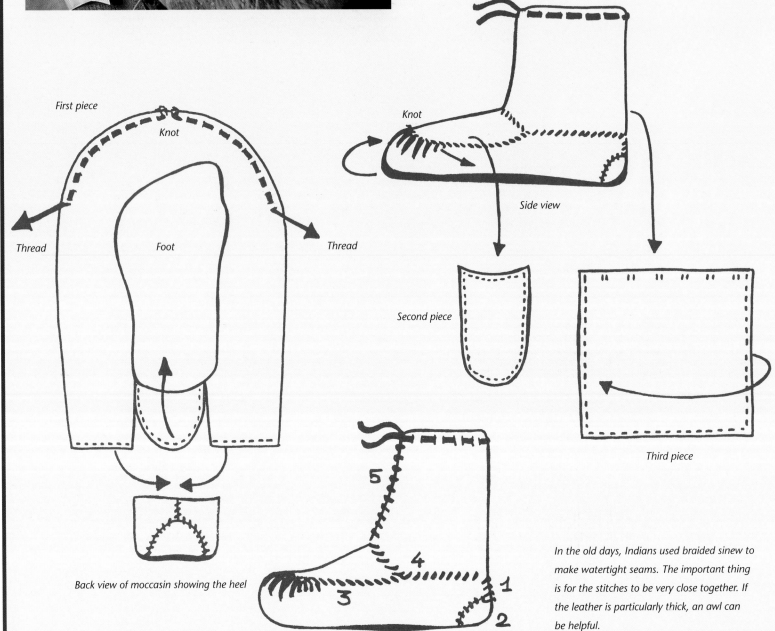

First piece

Knot

Thread

Foot

Thread

Knot

Side view

Second piece

Third piece

Back view of moccasin showing the heel

5

4

3

1

2

The seams are sewn in this order.

In the old days, Indians used braided sinew to make watertight seams. The important thing is for the stitches to be very close together. If the leather is particularly thick, an awl can be helpful.

There are many ways to attach a snowshoe to a moccasin. The method shown at right is the Montagnais method, which uses an elk hide strap to make a secure binding.

Fur or Freeze

Nothing is more beautiful than fur and nothing is warmer when it comes to protecting yourself from the cold. For Montaine, we sewed a beaverskin coat, a pair of coyote fur socks, and moosehide moccasins. In this outfit, she could stay outdoors for hours without complaining of the cold, even when the temperature was –40° F.

We waited a long time for the country around us to freeze solid, particularly the lake, which a thin layer of ice prevented us from canoeing on. The dogs, seeing the sled waiting in readiness, also were eager to be traveling over the frozen snow.

*Otchum, our lead dog, was no ordinary animal.
He had often proved this to us in Siberia,
Lapland, and France, and now he did so again
in Canada. He was extraordinarily tender and
affectionate toward Montaine; as long as he was
with her, nothing could happen to our daughter,
and the same was true for Diane and me. Once,
when we came across a grizzly, Otchum risked
his life to save mine. He deserves a whole book
to himself.*

Lake trout, or namaycush, can weigh up to forty pounds. In "our" lake, we caught several three-foot-long twenty-pounders. We divided them into eleven portions—one for each of the dogs and one for us.

The Long Journey Across the Yukon with Montaine

MOUNTAINS and more mountains. To the farthest point on the horizon, nothing but an ocean of mountain peaks. Whiteness everywhere, only relieved at the very bottom of the slumbering valleys by the green of the forest. The silence is total, oppressive, and inhuman, so thoroughly does it exclude all movement and heat, the essence of life. Everything is stopped, silent, frozen. The rivers and torrents, whose silvery dance lends the landscape life, are also asleep, arrested by the winter that has frozen this Far Northern land to its entrails. There is no trail, no glow of a lamp anywhere in the wan twilight. Hours pass, and the miles go by.

On the far side of a pass similar to a thousand others the plane has already overflown, the mountain below falls away and a valley appears in the evening shadow. Same whiteness, same vast silent spaces, same infinite solitude. Suddenly, the straight lines of a trail can be seen on the motionless river. And at the end of the trail, there

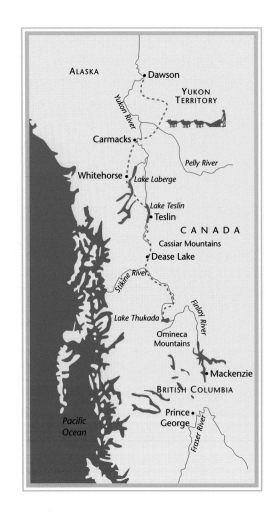

are dogs pulling a sled. A cloud of frost crystals surrounds them like a gray mist pouring out of their broad muzzles. In front of the dogs, a man wearing large snowshoes tamps down the deep, powdery snow. A woman walks behind the sled, where, bundled up in thick furs, a little girl sleeps. Her breath condenses in the freezing air to form a mist that joins the mist made by the dogs and by her mother behind her. The man and the woman walk without speaking, intent on the effort they are making, saving their breath. Their progress is slow and silent, in keeping with the landscape around them, so that they appear like tiny ants in a universe peopled by giants. Yet they stop when the plane passes overhead, making a yellow line in the metallic evening sky. They listen to the silence, suddenly inhabited by a noise. They look at the sky, where they suddenly see a movement they have not produced. Then the plane disappears. The silence returns, heavier and more total than before.

Below a certain temperature,

one is no longer cold—one is *in* the cold.

To avoid open sections of the river, we sometimes had to make long detours deep into the forest. Progress was very slow. We had to chop down trees to straighten the course, then push, pull, and free the sled, and finally make a trail in the deep snow by passing back and forth on it several times so that the dogs would be able to haul the sled and its heavy load. During the first part of our long trip, we would set off in the morning with nothing but the tent, the camp stove, and whatever Diane and Montaine needed for the night. As soon as we had stopped for the day, I would take seven dogs (the other three would stay in camp to rest) and go back along our trail, which was now well marked and often frozen hard, to pick up the load that we had left at our previous camp.

Montaine is taking a fascinating course in nature study, although the forest

seems to her the greatest playground in the world. Her little voice echoes commandingly across the silence,

calling each dog by name: Ouklok, Voulk, Kourvik, Baikal. . . . This is her way of counting to ten.

And the animals, growing docile at the sound, prick up their ears and one by one lengthen their pace,

responding to the wishes of their little mistress. This is Christmas for the snow child Montaine,

a Christmas such as every child in the world might dream of, total wonderment.

Freeze-Up and Breakup on a River

Autumn is no season for traveling. You have to wait for the rivers to freeze before you can go anywhere. The trick is in determining how thick the ice is, and any mistake can put you in serious danger. The first indication is the color of the ice—if it is black or gray it will be too thin to support you—and the next is the sound it makes when you tap its surface with a stick. But there are no sure rules or guidelines, and the only teacher is experience.

If the ice is at all questionable, prudence dictates following along the shoreline.

How a Very Fast-Flowing River Freezes

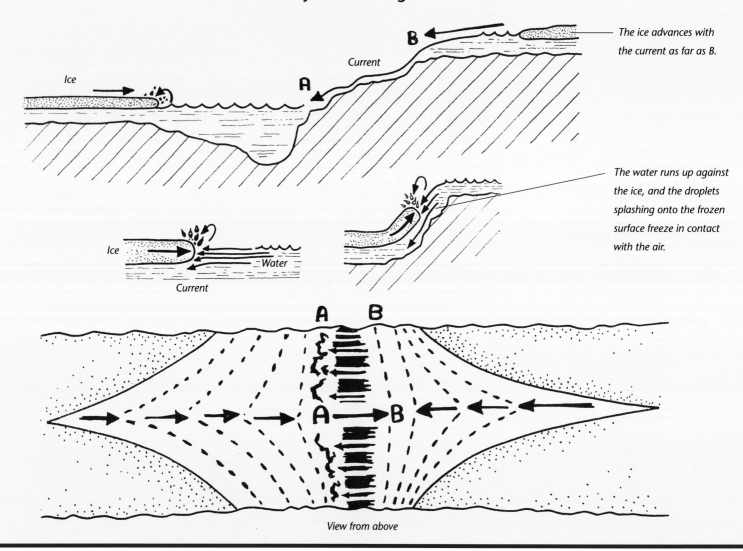

The ice advances with the current as far as B.

The water runs up against the ice, and the droplets splashing onto the frozen surface freeze in contact with the air.

View from above

The Dogsled's Path

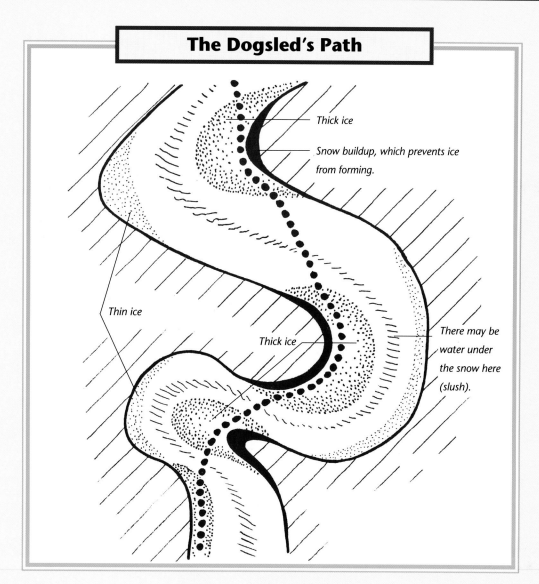

Thick ice

Snow buildup, which prevents ice from forming.

Thin ice

Thick ice

There may be water under the snow here (slush).

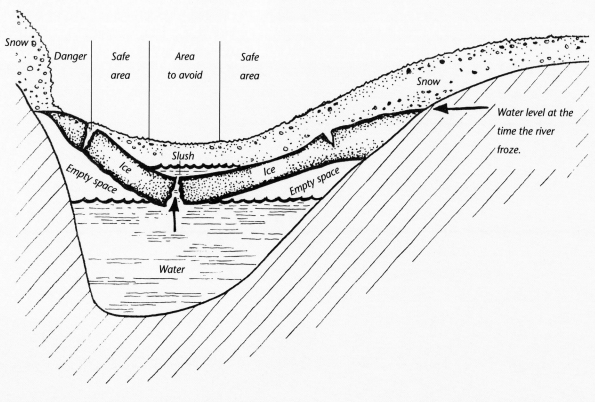

Snow

Danger

Safe area

Area to avoid

Safe area

Snow

Water level at the time the river froze.

Empty space

Ice

Slush

Ice

Empty space

Water

One way to save weight on an expedition is to hunt for your meat. But you can't spend too much time looking for game. Whatever happens, you just have to keep moving. Don't stop for too long when it's time to feed the dogs.

To Montaine, the forest is

the greatest playground in the world.

On the sled, Montaine stayed warm thanks to a small coal-fueled heater, but in the evening, her hands often grew cold, and she warmed them by the stove.

By the end of our expedition, Montaine and Otchum were on such close terms that she could hitch him to a sled and take off on a walk with him, calling out directions. Otchum followed her commands, always understanding them perfectly, even when her pronunciation was less than perfect: "gee" (for right), "yap" (for "haw," or left), and "hoo" (for "whoa").

The Wolf

Hunting in a Valley

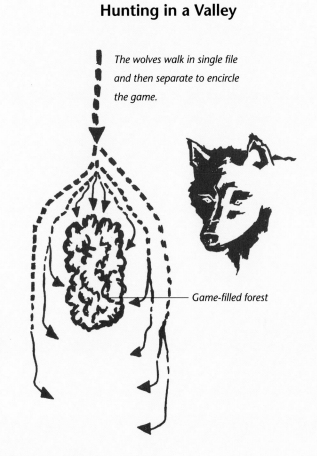

The wolves walk in single file and then separate to encircle the game.

Game-filled forest

In Canada, the magazine *Field and Stream* has offered a $1,000 prize for the last twenty years to anyone who can prove that a person has been attacked by a wolf or wolves. No one has ever claimed the prize. The only known case occurred in Montana in 1888! A young girl was bitten by a wolf, which was then shot and proved to have rabies.

World Distribution of the Wolf

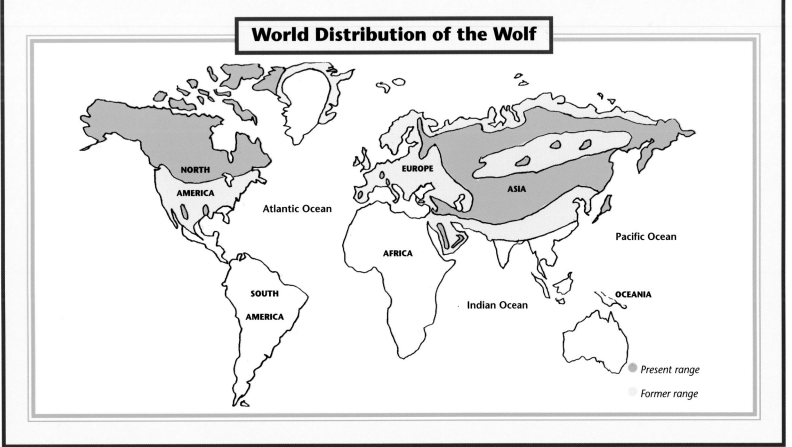

NORTH AMERICA

Atlantic Ocean

EUROPE

ASIA

AFRICA

Pacific Ocean

Indian Ocean

SOUTH AMERICA

OCEANIA

Present range

Former range

No more than a bluish bite mark on the deep ice covering, a fragile vein that fades into the vast sleeping landscape, the river stretches painfully over the frigid earth, silent and cold. Over its frozen waves a sled glides slowly, its runners squealing on the unmoving swells, which shatter and break. A man and a woman drive forward on snowshoes through the wind-borne snow, calling out encouragement to the dog team, which is led by a sturdy black-and-white Siberian husky. Nestled in the back of the wooden sled, a little girl nods in the warmth of her beaver-fur coat. Slowly she opens her eyes. Her bright glance seeks out Otchum, the lead dog, straining in the snow about twelve feet ahead of her, as he follows in the silver wake of his master. Laughing, she imitates the man's terse commands to his dog team. "Hooo!" she burbles. Her little voice, which has recently learned to mimic the song of chickadees and warblers, makes a musical moment that the wind carries off into the next frozen plain.

Pascal Paillardet,
from an article in *La Vie* magazine

Acknowledgments

I extend thanks to those of my teammates who used my cameras during the course of our expeditions and took the photographs in which I appear. They are, in alphabetical order: Thomas Bounoure, Benoît Maury-Laribière, Alain Rastoin, Nicolas Tozi, and Diane Vanier.

I would also like to express my gratitude to my editors, without whom this book would never have come about.

My thanks as well to all those who made my journeys possible: Pedigree Pal, Air Canada, Pinault, the Canadian Embassy, AB, Chlorophyle, TBF, Au Vieux Campeur, and the media, who have given me their confidence and support.

Designed by Rampazzo & Associates
Drawings and sketches by Nicolas Gilles
Project Coordinator, English-language edition: Ellen Rosefsky Cohen
Editor, English-language edition: Sharon AvRutick
Design Coordination, English-language edition: Dirk Luykx and Tina Thompson

Library of Congress Cataloging-in-Publication Data

Vanier, Nicolas.
    [Nord. English]
    North : adventures in the frozen wild / by Nicolas Vanier ; translated from the French by Willard Wood.
        p.   cm.
    Published simultaneously in the original French as: Nord : grands voyages dans les pays d'en haut.
    ISBN 0–8109–1391–7
    1. Vanier, Nicolas—Journeys.   2. Adventure and adventurers—Cold regions.
    3. Cold regions—Discovery and exploration.   I. Title.
    G530.V37V3613 1997
    910'.911—dc21   97–22000

Harry N. Abrams, Inc.
100 Fifth Avenue
New York, N.Y. 10011
www.abramsbooks.com